Dinner
PAWsible

D1565283

Dinner
PAWsible

A COOKBOOK OF NUTRITIOUS, HOMEMADE MEALS

for Cats and Dogs

CATHY ALINOVI, DVM,
and
SUSAN THIXTON

Skyhorse Publishing

Copyright © 2011 and 2015 by Cathy Alinovi and Susan Thixton

All rights reserved. No part of this book may be reproduced in any manner without the express written consent of the publisher, except in the case of brief excerpts in critical reviews or articles. All inquiries should be addressed to Skyhorse Publishing, 307 West 36th Street, 11th Floor, New York, NY 10018.

Skyhorse Publishing books may be purchased in bulk at special discounts for sales promotion, corporate gifts, fund-raising, or educational purposes. Special editions can also be created to specifications. For details, contact the Special Sales Department, Skyhorse Publishing, 307 West 36th Street, 11th Floor, New York, NY 10018 or info@skyhorsepublishing.com.

Skyhorse® and Skyhorse Publishing® are registered trademarks of Skyhorse Publishing, Inc.®, a Delaware corporation.

Visit our website at www.skyhorsepublishing.com.

10 9 8 7 6 5 4 3 2

Library of Congress Cataloging-in-Publication Data is available on file.

Cover design by Erin Seaward-Hiatt
Cover photograph: Thinkstock

Print ISBN: 978-1-63220-674-9
Ebook ISBN: 978-1-63220-919-1

Printed in China

To all members of our four-legged family—
you deserved this from the beginning.

TABLE OF CONTENTS

FOREWORD

The pet food industry has brainwashed us to think that we are not capable of feeding our own pets. Although we feed ourselves and our children every day, they have told us that we are somehow not capable of feeding our furry families. This is simply not true.

While there are many quality commercial pet foods on the market, the greatest majority of pet foods are made from inferior ingredients (as compared to food ingredients you'd purchase at the grocery store) and are highly processed. Regulations within the pet food industry have redefined ingredients used in pet food, causing them to have different meanings compared to what is commonly understood and accepted as food. For example, according to pet food regulations, the ingredient "chicken" may consist only of chicken skin and bones, or it could consist of chicken parts rejected for use in human food (DOA or diseased animals). The more pet food consumers learn about commercial pet food, the more they realize that it is worth it to cook for their pets, treating them in the same way as any other member of the family.

But then, fear sets in. What if I'm doing something wrong? What if I don't give them all the nutrients they need? What if I make them sick? What if…what if…what if?

I had that same fear too. But I assure you, it passes. As my intelligent and skilled co-author, Dr. Cathy, told me at the beginning of my transition from commercial pet food to home cooked: It's just food, so don't worry! The more you prepare their food, the more confidence you will have. Remember, you've been misled for years (maybe decades) that pet food only comes in the form of kibble or can. But soon, you are going to see just how wrong that information really is.

What about reports that home-prepared foods don't meet the nutritional requirements of cats and dogs?

A 2013 study performed by several UC Davis researchers caused a great deal of concern for pet food consumers. The study claimed that nearly 100% of home-prepared recipes did not provide dogs with sufficient nutrition as established by the National Research Council (cat recipes were not analyzed). This study has two significant flaws.

One flaw was that the researchers used the incorrect level of Vitamin D in comparing recipes to National Research Council (NRC) data. The UC Davis study stated that dogs require "339 IU of Vitamin D" per day, when the NRC actually recommends "136 IU of Vitamin D" per day (based on 1000 kcal).

Secondly, and most significantly, the nutrient requirements for cats and dogs that everyone, including the UC Davis study, uses as a standard was developed by the NRC, most recently published in 2006. Because these nutrient requirements are used by pet food regulations and major pet food manufacturers, the foundation of the NRC research was based on commonly used commercial pet food ingredients, including the use of added supplements (often synthetic), to provide nutrition. In other words, the nutrient requirements for cats and dogs were established from common pet food ingredients such as genetically modified grains and rendered meat meals, which are sourced from meats that are rejected for human consumption. The nutrient requirements established by NRC were also based on these common ingredients being heavily processed into kibble and canned pet foods.

The truth is there are no established nutritional requirements for cats and dogs based on animal consumption of whole food ingredients as prepared in the home. The exact amount of protein, fat, vitamins, and minerals a cat or dog would need—sourced from lightly processed food, not supplements—has not been established through scientific research. However, we do know that trying to compare a powdered meat meal to a roasted chicken prepared in your own kitchen is like trying to compare apples and oranges—multiplied by ten. It can't be done.

All the recipes in this book are close to NRC requirements for cats and dogs. We firmly believe that providing a variety of nutrition acquired from real or lightly processed foods will provide your pet with the most optimal standards of nutrition.

—Susan Thixton

INTRODUCTION

Dr. Cathy Alinovi

Over the last few years, I've learned more and more about food and feeding our pets. As my vet practice became more and more holistic, I learned that holistic care meant treating the whole patient, not just the current issue. So, if a client brings in a dog with itchy skin, it means figuring out the root cause behind his irritable skin, which in turn is often attributed to food allergies. Holistic practice also means spending a lot of time educating the client so they understand what is going on and why it is happening, and can make good health decisions themselves for their pets. Reeducating people and reexamining their assumptions about pet food has been an interesting journey.

First, I tried to talk clients into buying superior quality dog foods. Some clients balked at the cost, others wanted to do even better than that. Others simply had adorable little dogs that hardly ate anything, so I thought why not just feed them "people food"? I started by suggesting that owners feed healthy people food to their dogs. To my surprise, some owners actually thought hot dogs and crackers were healthy! I was shocked; I thought everyone knew what constituted healthy food. So, I started writing down recipes.

Then, I had a client who lost several cats due to an unidentifiable something in the cat food. It wasn't melamine and it wasn't anything the FDA could find wrong, but the cats only fell sick when they ate that specific brand of food. My client was devastated. I was traumatized that all my efforts couldn't save those poor cats. We had to find a new way to feed her cats safely, healthily, and simply.

The other thing that motivated me was the belief that cooking for our pets should be fun. My favorite chef for people food, George Geary, makes cooking fun. I hope everyone has as much fun cooking for their pets as my husband and I have when we prepare George's recipes! Every morning and night, I line up all the dog dishes (usually ten to fifteen dishes in total, especially when I include some of my hospitalized guests), fight the cats off the serving bowl, and dish out a pretty healthy meal. It's fun and exciting for me; and my crew sure is excited as well!

Dr. Cathy and Max

Dr. Cathy and I met when a client of hers lost several cats, apparently due to a pet food problem (the story she shares on the previous pages). She reached out to me trying to find answers for her client. We hit it off immediately. Through many conversations, the idea of a pet food cookbook began.

I shared with Dr. Cathy stories of my grandparents having healthy, long-living dogs and cats that ate nothing but table scraps (and the occasional mouse captured by the cat). Dr. Cathy shared with me that she cooks for her own pets and even hospitalized pets in her clinic (if the situation allows). We both agreed that healthy food makes for healthy pets—thus the cooking began. There is a joy that is difficult to describe that comes from putting wholesome foods together to create a homemade meal for your pet. To watch them savor every bite and clean the bowl, and to know that I made it for them from scratch. It is a tremendous feeling—you'll see.

Cooking takes just a little time and getting used to (of course this could just be me—I didn't cook much before this). But, as you are about to find out, it is well worth the effort. You'll know exactly what your pet is eating! How great is that?

Susan Thixton and Kirby

Top left: Beans, photo courtesy of Kayla Young
Top right: Zoe, photo courtesy of Aubrey King
Bottom left: Dakotah Superstar, photo courtesy of Barbara Slegers-Hudson
Bottom right: Kit Kat, photo courtesy of Aubrey King

THE CASE FOR MAKING YOUR OWN PET FOOD

Certainly, it is easier to just go to the store and purchase a bag of kibble for your pet. But those who decide to prepare pet food at home aren't looking for the easiest way to feed their pet—they are looking for the healthiest. Each year, dozens to hundreds of commercial pet foods are recalled and thousands of pets suffer permanent injury (such as kidney or liver disease) or even death. Most controversially, in 2007 thousands of dogs and cats were hospitalized and even killed due to a wide-scale contamination in pet food. Melamine, a cheap and toxic pet food additive, caused fatal kidney failure resulting in, reportedly, as many as 3,600 deaths. Over 5,000 pet food products were recalled.

On the contrary, pet deaths are rarely linked directly to home-made food, save for a handful of documented illnesses, over many, many years. Is there really that much of a difference between commercial pet food and home-prepared foods?

In most cases, there is a huge difference. We'll look at three significant elements: production scale, supplements, and ingredient quality.

Mass production

Most commercial pet foods are made in massive batches, such as 8,000-pound batches (kibble), with some being even larger. The raw ingredients are loaded into a large mixer, powdered, and liquid vitamin and mineral pre-mixes are added in. This raw dough is pressed through a tube while being cooked under heat and pressure. The dough is cut at the end of the tube into kibble shapes and dried through more heat. Flavorings are sprayed on as a final step.

Have you ever wondered why so many vitamins and minerals are added to pet foods? If the pet food contained real meat, vegetables, and fruits, wouldn't the natural nutrients in these ingredients be sufficient nutrition for the pet? They would, under normal circumstances, but because the cooking process of kibble is so extensive, most of the nutrients in the ingredients are destroyed. This is why most kibble pet foods have so many vitamins and minerals added back in. Almost all the natural nutrients from the raw ingredients have been destroyed during the extrusion process.

With home-prepared food, you control the cooking. Ingredients are roasted or steamed and never overcooked. The nutrients remain in the food for your pet to feast and nourish themselves on.

One more concern of mass production is mixing. When you bake a cake at home, it's hard to get all the lumps out, isn't it? Well, lumps in a 8,000-pound batch of pet food occur too. Those lumps could cause a serious health concern for the pet consuming them. In that 8,000-pound (or larger) batch of pet food, powdered vitamins and minerals are also added in. If these vitamins and minerals are not distributed evenly throughout the mix, the pet is at risk of consuming a large dose of a certain vitamin or mineral, which could be toxic. When your pet's food is made at home, there is no concern of accidental toxic overdosing of supplements.

Supplements

With home-prepared food, 100% of your pet's necessary nutrition is provided by natural ingredients that come straight from your kitchen, besides calcium (due to how all foods are reared, calcium is no longer naturally occurring in high concentrations, and we either need to eat more cheese or add a calcium supplement).

In contrast, most commercial pet foods rely on nutrition from added supplements. A term in nutrition we must consider is bio-availability, which means (in simple terms) how the body absorbs and utilizes the nutrients it receives. The goal with nutrition is to provide nutrients that are very bio-available; nutrients that the body easily recognizes and utilizes.

Home-prepared pet foods excel in bio-availability. Our recipes use food, not supplements, to provide 100% of your pets' nutritional needs. Even our calcium source comes from natural food—eggshell or seaweed.

Quality of Ingredients

The biggest difference between most commercial pet foods and home-prepared pet foods is the quality of the ingredients. The food that humans consume (ingredients you'll purchase at your local grocery store) must abide by different laws, including passing USDA inspection, warehousing laws, and even transportation laws (to the grocery or restaurant). The food that animals and pets consume does not. In fact, animal foods are allowed to contain some of the worst wastes imaginable, with no laws in place to inform consumers of the food's true content.

Meat and vegetable ingredients that are rejected for use in human food are part of this waste. Expired meats, expired frozen dinners, and even used restaurant grease are not discarded.

All of this waste is welcome to be used in pet foods, with no disclosure to the pet food consumer. One of the worst wastes is the rejected meat product known as 4D, with each D standing for Dead, Diseased, Dying, and Disabled. 4D animals—such as cattle that have died in the field or diseased poultry—would not be processed into human food, but are welcome in pet food. Again, consumers are not informed if their pet foods are made with 4D meats or any other waste foods. Labels on a bag or a can may display pretty images of choice cuts of meats and fresh vegetables, but inside the bag the food is made of horrible waste that no pet owner would consider to be food.

Preparation of foods in the home is how pet owners can guarantee that what they want to be in their pets' food is indeed in the food.

Look how unappetizing can food and kibble look! As you begin preparing home-cooked foods for your pets, you will slowly remove these unhealthy commercial pet foods from their diets.

As we try to set up Echo and his dinner for a picture, Mikey the cat leaps onto the table and greedily steals his home-prepared meal.

BUT I BARELY HAVE TIME TO COOK FOR MYSELF...

Boy, do we understand the feeling of not having the time to cook for anybody! Collectively, we feed real food to nine dogs, twenty-three cats and two birds (current count) every day. Both of us also run our own businesses and often work twelve- to fourteen-hour days, so we can relate to being overwhelmed by having to cook. On the other hand, because we are real food zealots, in an ideal world we want to make all the food for our dogs and cats, every meal, every day. But we also understand the realities of life! While we would love you to build up to daily home-prepared meals for your pets, even if you start off by feeding them just *one* real meal a week, you will already be doing great things for your dogs and cats.

Imagine: you lead such a busy life that you are forced to get all of your meals from fast food restaurants. For some of us, this isn't so far from real life. However, once a week during Sunday brunch, you dedicate time to cook yourself a good meal of homemade, healthy food, and it's the best meal of your week. You feel great, you have good energy, your tummy digests well, and it's just an overall enjoyable experience. Well, it's the same thing for your dogs and cats. If once a week is all you can muster, then that is what it will be.

The great thing about starting with one home-cooked meal a week is that you will learn to get the feel of preparing recipes. Because a lot of people don't cook for themselves anymore, the idea of cooking for their pets makes them feel inadequate in the kitchen. Fortunately, most of our dogs are not that finicky and they won't give us negative feedback. Instead, most dogs devour the food we give them and ask for more, soothing our challenged egos and letting us know that we have done the right thing. Cats, well, cats are cats and may be picky for a while, but with persistence, offering little tasty homemade treats will eventually win most cats over. Once you get the hang of cooking once a week, you will build up more confidence. The next time you find free time during a week of vacation, prepare more recipes.

It has taken our families some time to figure it out. We use two slow cookers, and at least one is going 70% of the time. We have not fed our nine dogs commercial dog food since we first wrote this book. It can be done!

Even if you use the recipes in this book just to make treats or to perform a liver detoxification for your pet after an annual vaccine, it is still a great start. You are taking small steps to make your dog's or cat's life better. That home-cooked meal, even if only once a week, will nourish every living tissue and fiber in your pet's body better than any other commercial pet foods. Just one home-prepared meal a week is going to make your beloved friend happy. Your dog will lick your face and dance around the food dish more than ever before; your cat's hairballs will be reduced and her drive to drink water will lessen.

Every pet owner wants to do everything they can to improve their furry friends' lives, but it also has to fit into their busy lifestyle.

Some pet owners work too much to cook at home, while others will stay up late to make sure it happens. All we ask is that you do your best. It's what your pets ask of you. And if you eventually go whole hog and dive in to make every meal yourself, you are getting that much closer to ensuring great health for your pets!

Beans and Gunny, photo courtesy of Kayla Young

MAKING THE CHANGE FROM COMMERCIAL TO HOMEMADE

Until now, you've probably been feeding your pet commercial food. Switching over to home-prepared food takes a little getting used to. You need to learn a few things first, and so does your pet.

Try to imagine only eating fast food ever since you were born—your body and your taste buds get very familiar with the consistency, flavor, and even particulars like the saltiness of the food. One day, after years of gorging on fast food, imagine eating a home-cooked pasta dinner, complete with meatballs and fresh tomato sauce. For starters, you wouldn't know how to eat pasta because you've never had it before. Secondly, your 'insides' are not yet used to the fresh ingredients, including all the good nutrition from the home-cooked meal. It would take some time getting used to. Well, this works the same for your dog and cat.

If they have been eating kibble all their life, they might not know how to eat 'real food' at first. Some will give you a look that seems to say, "This is a joke, right?" "This is a set-up and you're going to yell at me next for stealing your food, right?" The cats who have eaten nothing but kibble their entire lives (please try to get them on soft food!) might look at their new home-cooked meal disdainfully: "This time the joke's on you if you think I'm going to eat this!"

Fortunately, it only takes time. Most dogs quickly learn to eat home-prepared food, and cats who put up an initial struggle can ultimately be lured in with the addition of broth. For kibble-addicted cats, you can grind some kibble in a food processor and sprinkle kibble powder over their home-prepared meal.

If you plan to introduce home-cooked food to cats who have previously been on kibble diets, remove the kibble gradually. It is more important to ensure that your cat eats every single day, so go back to kibble or canned if they do not eat home-cooked food regularly (a meal every twelve hours is preferred). If cats begin eating home-prepared food from the start, no gradual introduction is needed.

For dogs, an abrupt change from kibble or canned to home-cooked food can cause loose stools and upset tummies. Begin with a ratio of three parts commercial food to one part home-cooked for three to four days. Then progress to equal parts over three to four days, and so on. Dogs who have consistently been snuck 'people food' treats should have an easy transition and will probably not suffer from intestinal upset.

There are adjustments that pet parents need to make when shifting to home-prepared pet foods too. The obvious adjustment is preparation. Proper planning is necessary to have ingredients on hand and sufficient time to prepare the food. A food processor, a coffee grinder (for eggshell calcium), and a slow cooker are helpful tools.

The other adjustment pet parents need to make is in their attitudes. Pet parents have been brainwashed by the pet food industry. We have been programmed to believe that our pets should only eat commercially-prepared kibble or canned food that provides a 100% nutritionally balanced meal. This belief system we rely on is not completely correct. Yes, our pets must have a balance of necessary nutrients in their diet. But no, this balance does not have to be reached during each meal. Balance of nutrition can be easily achieved with a variety of food (each food providing a variety of nutrients) over weeks or months. Mother Nature has designed all of us (our pets included) to be seasonal eaters. This can be seen in the different seasons in nature that provide a wide selection of foods (spring crops, summer crops, and so on). Man and beast have depended on these seasonal varieties, long before there was any commercial pet food, to take in all the nutrition we need in order to thrive. Not a completely balanced nutritional intake at each meal at the expense of quality food, but quality nutrition obtained through a variety of whole foods over time.

Let's look at how two identical recipes, when executed in different ways, have incredibly varied nutritional values.

Two chefs make a meatloaf. Chef A uses freshly ground chuck, homemade bread crumbs, a fresh tomato, and fresh spices from the garden. Chef B isn't so particular. Chef B finds a package of frozen ground beef in the freezer. It might be freezer burnt, but it's beef, so who cares? Chef B finds some bread crumbs in the pantry, a can of chopped tomatoes, and uses spices that could be years old. Each meatloaf contains identical ingredients, but they are drastically different from a nutritional standpoint.

Chef A cooks his meatloaf at 325 degrees until just done in thirty minutes. Chef B isn't so picky. Chef B's meatloaf is cooked at 400 degrees for an hour; he wants to make sure it is good and done but doesn't have time to check it constantly. Again, each meatloaf contains identical ingredients; however much of the nutrition would be destroyed in Chef B's meatloaf due to overcooking.

This example emphasizes the problem with commercial pet food industry's nutrient requirements for cats and dogs. The established nutrient requirements are based on 'commonly used' commercial pet food ingredients such as a by-product meal made with meats that have been rejected for use in human food—similar to the ingredients used by Chef B. Furthermore, these 'common' pet food ingredients are then cooked under pressure and heat to an extent that almost all of the nutrients are destroyed. This is why most commercial pet foods contain so many added vitamins and minerals, because the nutrients in the original ingredients are nonexistent due to the poor quality of the ingredients and the heavy cooking.

On the other hand, home-prepared pet foods that follow the exact same recipe will have a higher nutritional value, featuring nutrients that occur naturally in the food. Our recipes follow the established nutritional guidelines for cats and dogs, and promise to provide more wholesome nutrients than commercial pet foods ever will. Although a single recipe will not meet all nutritional requirements exactly, eating from a variety of recipes over an extended period of time will ensure adequate variety. This is the way Mother Nature intended for our pets to obtain all the nutrients they need. Plus, real food is easily absorbed by the body.

Some pet parents feed their pets commercial food in the morning and home-prepared meals in the evening. Others feed half portions of home-prepared food and commercial food each meal. Others feed home-prepared foods exclusively. It's up to you—whatever works best for you and your pet.

COOKING WITH VARIETY

You have learned the basic preparation steps for each ingredient. Now, here is the most important piece of information you'll need to know about home-prepared pet food:

VARIETY, VARIETY, VARIETY

It is easier to provide variety to dogs. Cats can be a little more challenging. Susan's cats are a great example. One eats everything (he even steals vegetables out of the dog food bowl). The other two are pickier. One of her finicky eaters doesn't care much for beef, but loves fish. She'll eat chicken very well, likes turkey, but refuses ground turkey recipes. Susan's other picky eater loves chicken, beef, and turkey, but is not too keen on clams, oysters, or sardines. However, he loves salmon! Sometimes, it is helpful to put home-prepared cat food back into the food processor to blend it one more time. Many cats seem to prefer finely ground food. However, the good news is that they all love broth. They will pay attention to any food with broth, even the meats they don't usually prefer. So, with the help of broth, even picky cats will have the benefit of a variety of meat proteins.

Examples of a meal plan with variety are:

Week One
Monday and Tuesday—Beef Stroganoff (pg 150)
Wednesday and Thursday—Clam Chowder (pgs 120 & 174)
Friday and Saturday—Turkey Meatloaf (pgs 96 & 142)
Sunday—Chicken & Clams (pg 124)

Week Two
Monday and Tuesday—Turkey, Shrimp and Black Beans
(pg 137)
Wednesday and Thursday—Chicken & Seafood (pg 132)
Friday and Saturday—Duck Casserole (pgs 103 & 146)
Sunday—Steak & Eggs (pg 109)

By using a wide selection of recipes every week, you will be providing your pet with a balanced and interesting diet.

No one meal within this cookbook is perfectly balanced (though all of them come very close). Some might have a little more B vitamins than others, some recipes might be a little lower in potassium or zinc according to the NRC recommended daily feeding guidelines, while others might be higher. However, eating a variety of meals over a week or month will lead to a balanced diet for the consumer. The key to providing your pet with a healthy home-prepared diet is by utilizing various ingredients and foods over a period of time.

Which would you rather eat: canned food and kibble, or fresh ingredients such as these mushrooms, string beans, squash, and ground chicken? Well, your pet would think the same!

PREPARING THE INGREDIENTS

Cooking for your pet is actually very easy! Apply the appropriate preparation technique listed here to any ingredient found in the recipes to make tasty, healthy pet food.

1. Preparation of meats
2. Preparation of organ meats
3. Preparation of vegetables and fruits
4. Preparation and/or selection of supplements
5. Preparation of broth

We've provided detailed information for each preparation technique in the following pages, and also explained the most economical ways to store and cook food for your pets. Note that the instructions to store portion sizes are based on the average ten-pound cat or the standard thirty-pound dog. If you have smaller or larger animals, adjust your portion sizes appropriately when storing.

1. Preparation of meats

The best meat for your pet is organic. The most cost-efficient way of obtaining organic meat is to purchase larger portions (beef) or the entire bird (chicken/turkey) at one go. If organic meat does not fit your budget, no worries. Regular meat is still a healthy option for your pet; it is certainly healthier than processed meats in canned or kibble pet foods.

Basically, you are going to cook meats using the simplest preparation methods—boiling, baking, or grilling. Seasoning is not a requirement, but it is a viable option (however, no onions). Seasonings have their own medicinal/digestive functions. If you chose to season your pets' food, do so lightly. Let's discuss each type of meat and your options of preparation.

Chicken We purchase chickens whole and prefer to boil them whole in a large pot. Chicken can also be roasted in the oven. Use a meat thermometer to ensure that the temperature on the inside is 185°F. Once the chicken is cooked, remove from water/oven and allow to cool.

Remove the fat, skin, and bones. Discard the fat and skin, but save bones for the broth.

Remove the meat and grind in a food processor. Combine light and dark meat into your grind. Dark meat from chicken has more fat and slightly less protein than white meat.

Store ground chicken in half-cup portions in the refrigerator (three days maximum), or freeze. Label each chicken portion properly with the name of the meat, amount, and date frozen, for example "Chicken ½ cup 5/1/15." The date on the package lets you know how long it has been frozen.

Keep the bones to make chicken stock or broth! See subsequent instructions on how to add flavor and nutrition to each recipe using homemade broth.

Beef Depending on the size of the piece of meat, you can grill or boil it. A slightly pink center is acceptable. Cut away fat and gristle, and discard. Chop or grind the meat in a food processor and store in half-cup portions. Refrigerate for three days (maximum) or freeze. Label each portion with the name of the meat, amount, and date frozen. Lean ground beef can also be used—fry in olive oil in a skillet until the pink is just gone, and drain grease (do not rinse the meat as this rinses away all nutrients).

Turkey Roasting turkey whole in the oven is the simplest way to prepare a turkey. Use a meat thermometer to ensure that internal temperature is 185°F. Remove the fat and skin of the cooked turkey and discard. Save bones for broth. Grind the meat in a food processor. Store in half-cup portions in the refrigerator (three days maximum) or freeze. Label each portion with the name of the meat, amount, and date frozen. Combine dark and light meat in your grind. If you purchase ground turkey directly, lightly fry in olive oil in skillet, and drain grease (do not rinse the meat as this rinses away all nutrients).

Fish Grill, bake, or simmer in water. Break up lightly with a fork and store in quarter-cup portions. Refrigerate for three days (maximum) or freeze. Label each portion with the name of the meat, amount, and date frozen.

Reminders Boil, roast, or grill meat until done, and always use a meat thermometer. Grind in food processor (for both dogs and cats) or chop into bite-size pieces (for dogs). Store in half-cup portions. Refrigerate for maximum of three days or freeze up to three months. Label each meat portion with the name of the meat, amount, and date frozen. How finely you grind the food will depend on the size of your pet.

2. Preparation of organ meats

It is difficult to find organic livers and hearts, but if you can locate them, they are your best choice. If organic organ meats are not available, purchasing regular organ meats from a grocery store or butcher shop are also healthy options.

Liver (either chicken or beef) Liver can be boiled or pan-fried. If you pan-fry, use a small amount of healthy oil such as olive oil, coconut oil, or butter. One tablespoon should be sufficient. Once cooled, grind ingredients (such as chicken livers OR beef liver, but don't combine them) in a food processor and store in two tablespoon portions. Refrigerate for three days (maximum) or freeze. Label each portion with the name of the meat, amount, and date frozen.

3. Preparation of vegetables and fruits

Again, you have the option of purchasing organic vegetables and fruits. For cats, vegetables and fruits should be finely ground or finely chopped; for dogs, vegetables and fruit should be chopped into bite-size pieces (depending on the size of your dog). All vegetables should be steamed or blanched, but not heavily. For our purposes, 'lightly cooked' refers to semi-soft vegetables. Apples can be served raw or steamed.

Reminders Chop vegetables into bite-sized pieces for dogs; grind finely for cats. Blanch vegetables until semi-cooked. Fruits can be raw or lightly blanched. Grind unsalted sunflower seeds until fine for cats.

4. Preparation and/or selection of supplements

Oil Cod liver oil should be purified. Any health food store would carry purified fish oils.

Tip: If you purchase cod liver oil in capsules, three 1000-mg capsules equal approximately one teaspoon. Simply snip one end of the capsule with scissors and squeeze the oil onto the food. Other oils can be substituted, such as olive, organic grape seed, or coconut.

Calcium Most of these recipes require a calcium supplement. Dr. Cathy prefers Essentials Seaweed Calcium, available online and at specialty pet stores, while Susan prefers ground eggshells as a calcium source. Each recipe in this book provides the required milligram of calcium needed.

To make eggshell calcium, dry the shells of six to twelve eggs in a 250-degree oven for twenty minutes. Grind shells in a coffee grinder until fine. Store unused eggshell powder in the refrigerator.

5. Preparation of broth

While broth or stock is an optional ingredient in each recipe, it adds wonderful flavor to home-prepared pet foods, as well as added nutrition. Broth is especially beneficial to cats (who tend to not drink enough water). We encourage you to add home-prepared broth to each recipe.

To prepare broth: save the bones from a cooked whole chicken or whole turkey. Place the bones into a slow cooker or the same large pot you cooked the chicken in. Add just enough water to cover the bones (approximately two cups of water per one pound of bones). Add two tablespoons of cider vinegar per pound of bones. Let stand for one hour. Bring to a low boil, reduce heat, and let simmer for six to twelve hours for chicken or turkey bones, and twelve to twenty-four hours for beef bones. Strain broth through a colander or sieve lined with cheesecloth. Discard bones. DO NOT feed these bones to your pet.

The broth can be refrigerated for three days or frozen. Freeze in eight- or sixteen-ounce containers (one- or two-cup capacity).

Tip: Never substitute canned broth for homemade broth. Canned broths often have high salt/sodium levels.

Reminders Cook bones in just enough water to cover. Add two tablespoons of vinegar per pound of bones. Simmer for approximately six hours and strain out solids. Refrigerate for a maximum of three days or freeze.

Lasagna for dogs prepared in bulk.

PREPARING RECIPES IN BULK

To help you make efficient use of your time, plan ahead and prepare your pet's food in bulk beforehand, in order to make more than a day's worth of food for an entire household. Recipes also need to be adjusted to larger quantities if your family has a dog that weighs more than thirty pounds or a cat that tips the scale at more than ten pounds.

For the purpose of this book, all our recipes are based on feeding the standard thirty-pound dog and ten-pound cat for a single day. Dogs obviously have large weight variations, from the teacup Yorkie to the giant English Mastiff. Most cats weigh from nine to twelve pounds; however there are some petite kitties that top the scale at six pounds and some hefty cats who weigh up to eighteen pounds. If your dog is lighter or heavier than thirty pounds and your cat lighter or heavier than ten pounds, portion modifications to the recipes will be necessary.

Additionally, feed your pet according to the weight they *should* be. This means that if your dog or cat is overweight, you want to feed them according to their ideal, not current, weight. For example, if you have a 106-pound German Shepherd who should weigh eighty pounds, feed him the amount needed for an eighty-pound pet and remember to use that number in your ingredient calculations.

Here is how to plan to cook a week's worth of food for the entire household at one go: come up with a multiplier. How much food to prepare over the course of a week depends on the number and sizes of your pets.

First, here is a table for dogs that you can use to come up with an appropriate multiplier.

A: Cumulative weight of dogs in household (lbs)	B: A x Number of days	C, your weekly multiplier: B ÷ 30 (rounded up)
90 + 10 + 40 = **140**	140 x 7 = **980**	980 ÷ 30 = **33**

A: For example, if you are a multiple-dog home, add the desired weights for all dogs together. For example, if you are cooking for a household consisting of a ninety-pound golden retriever, a ten-pound beagle, and a forty-pound standard poodle, you need to prepare food for **140** pounds of dog per day.

B: Next, if you plan to prepare food for everyone for a total of seven days, multiply the daily weight requirement of 140 by **7**, which equals **980**. If you intend to feed your pets homemade food every day, we recommend preparing food weekly.

C: Finally, since our recipes are written for a thirty-pound dog, the cumulative weight of 980 pounds of dog that has to be fed over seven days should be divided by 30, which equals **33**. In all cases, it's easier to round up to the nearest whole number.

Thus, **33** is your weekly multiplier. You will need thirty-three times the ingredients from our standard recipes to feed your entire canine family for seven days. So, whenever you prepare food in bulk, always remember to multiply the ingredient quantities by your multiplier. Adjust it whenever necessary, if you have additions to the family, or would like to prepare food for fewer or more days.

Here is the table for cats. If you have two cats, one weighing eight pounds and the other twelve pounds, and you would like to prepare food in bulk for the next five days, this is how to compute your multiplier:

A: Cumulative weight of cats in household (lbs)	B: A x Number of days	C, your weekly multiplier: B ÷ 10 (rounded up)
8 + 12 = **20**	20 x 5 = **100**	100 ÷ 10 = **10**

To prepare food for two cats over five days, you have to multiply all ingredient quantities by **10**.

When multiplying your ingredient quantities, you can round all fractions up to make things easier. Some numbers are also easier to understand if standard measurements like teaspoons and cups are converted to quarts or gallons for volume and pounds for weight. Here's a chart to help with the conversions:

Teaspoons	Tablespoon	Cup	Ounce	Pounds	Pint	Quart	Gallon
3	1	$1/16$	$1/2$	$1/32$	$1/32$	$1/64$	$1/256$
6	2	$1/8$	1	$1/16$	$1/16$	$1/32$	$1/128$
12	4	$1/4$	2	$1/8$	$1/8$	$1/16$	$1/64$
24	8	$1/2$	4	$1/4$	$1/4$	$1/8$	$1/32$
48	16	1	8	$1/2$	$1/2$	$1/4$	$1/16$
96	32	2	16	1	1	$1/2$	$1/8$
192	64	4	32	2	2	1	$1/4$
768	256	16	128	8	8	4	1

Taking the example of a canine family weighing a total of 140 pounds, to make seven days' worth of a recipe that calls for a half cup of chicken, multiply ½ cup by the multiplier of 33 to get 16 ½ cups of chicken. According to this chart, 16 cups is a gallon (or 8 pounds). Therefore, you will need a gallon plus half a cup (8 ¼ pounds) of chicken.

For some readers, these calculations come naturally. For those who are easily confused by the math, there are reasonably priced Smartphone applications that will convert recipes for you, so don't stress! Have patience and follow the recipe steps.

As a last resort, you can always ballpark a recipe prepared in bulk. This is food, not rocket science! With practice and confidence, quantities can be estimated and rounded up for large batches.

If you feed your pet a variety of different recipes over a couple of weeks, you will provide your pet with a variety of nutrition. As long as you stay close to the estimated proportions of meats, organ meats, fibers, and vitamins or minerals in a recipe, your pet should be fine.

Portion Estimator

For cats—meats and organ meats make up approximately 80–85% of any recipe (higher percentage of meat, lesser of organ meat). Approximately 10–15% is fat, and 5% makes up carbohydrate ingredients that provide vitamins, minerals, and fiber.

For dogs—meats and organ meats make up approximately 25–50% of any recipe (higher percentage of meat, lesser of organ meat). Approximately 10–15% is fat, and 35–65% (remainder) carbohydrate ingredients that provide vitamins, minerals and fiber.

Freezing and Warming

All of these recipes freeze well, as do the individual ingredients. Simply allow food to thaw before serving. Do not microwave in plastic as toxins will be released from the plastic.

While cold leftover pizza can be quite tasty, hot pizza right out of the oven is the *best*. The same holds true for your pet with home-prepared food. Some pets have no issue with refrigerated pet food, while others do. For the pet that prefers a warm meal, add a small amount of hot water (or broth) to the food and mix well, or microwave the food in a microwave-safe dish (no plastic!) for ten to fifteen seconds and stir well. Microwaves often cause hot spots in food, so be very careful with them as they could burn your pet.

Come up with your own multiplier

FOR DOGS

A: Cumulative weight of dogs in household (lbs)	B: A x Number of days	C, your weekly multiplier: B ÷ 30 (rounded up)

FOR CATS

A: Cumulative weight of cats in household (lbs)	B: A x Number of days	C, your weekly multiplier: B ÷ 10 (rounded up)

HEALTH BENEFITS OF EACH INGREDIENT

MEATS

Beef Grass-fed beef is a quality protein source that also provides a good source of B vitamins, selenium, zinc, iron, and phosphorus.

Beef Liver Beef liver provides pets with a quality source of iron, B12, riboflavin, zinc, copper, folate, selenium, niacin, and phosphorus. Organic liver, if available, is best.

Chicken Chicken is a quality protein source that also supplies niacin and selenium to the diet.

Chicken Liver Chicken liver provides a quality source of vitamin A, folate, vitamin B12, and iron. Organic liver, if available, is best.

Clams Clams are a quality protein source for your pet that also provides an excellent source of iron. Clams also provide phosphorus, potassium, zinc, copper, and manganese.

Duck Duck provides meat protein as well as a good source of phosphorus, selenium, and various B vitamins.

Mackerel Similar to sardines, mackerel is a great protein source providing a significant variety of vitamins, minerals, and healthy omega-3 fatty acids. Mackerel with bone provides a good source of calcium.

Salmon Pink and chum varieties provide a great source of healthy omega-3 fatty acids. Salmon is also a great protein source, rich in vitamin D, B3 (niacin), and B12. Salmon with bones included (example canned pink salmon) is also a great source of calcium.

Sardines Sardines are a great protein source that provides significant vitamin B3, B12 and D, selenium, and healthy omega-3 fatty acids. Sardines are also a good source of phosphorus and calcium.

Shrimp Shrimp are low fat, high in protein, and an excellent source of selenium. They are also a good source of vitamin D, B12, and healthy omega-3 fatty acids.

Turkey Turkey provides an alternative meat protein source for your pet as well as providing selenium, vitamin B3 and B6, phosphorus, and zinc.

VEGETABLES AND FRUIT

Acorn Squash Acorn squash contains vitamin A, niacin, folate, thiamine, and vitamin B6, but is also a great source of vitamin C. This squash also provides magnesium and potassium (which helps maintain the body's water balance). In addition, acorn squash is one of the best sources of beta carotene (antioxidant).

Alfalfa Sprouts Alfalfa sprouts are the only plant that supplies the full range of vitamins—from vitamin A, B complex, C, and E to vitamin K. They also contain calcium, folic acid, magnesium, manganese, molybdenum, phosphorus, potassium, and zinc. Sprouts are rich in antioxidants and provide inflammation-inhibiting compounds.

Apple Apples supply quality fiber to your pets' diet as well as many phytonutrients that provide anti-inflammatory protection and disease prevention. Recent studies show anti-cancer benefits in apples.

Asparagus Research has shown that asparagus contains saponins that have anti-inflammatory and anti-cancer properties. Saponins in food are also associated with improved blood pressure and better control of blood fat levels. This vegetable contains inulin, which is a prebiotic and may help the digestive tract. Asparagus is a wonderful source of vitamin K, folate, copper, selenium, and various vitamins.

Beans–Black and Red Black and red beans are an excellent source of folate, fiber, manganese, magnesium, iron, phosphorus, and vitamin B1 (thiamin). Black and red beans are also an excellent source of the trace mineral molybdenum, which is responsible for detoxifying sulfites (a type of preservative commonly added to prepared foods). Black and red beans are rich in antioxidants, equal to the antioxidant powers of fruits such as blueberries. Animal studies suggest that not only do black beans help protect against cancer, but a "clear reduction" in the number of pre-cancerous cells were seen in those with these beans in their diet. Studies have also shown that black and red beans help prevent heart disease.

Broccoli Broccoli provides a high amount of vitamin C, which aids iron absorption. It also provides a good source of folic acid and potassium. Broccoli is a fiber-rich food. The sulforaphane in broccoli helps to increase the level of enzymes that block cancer, while the beta-carotene in broccoli transforms into vitamin A, providing an effective antioxidant that destroys free radicals.

Brown Rice Brown rice provides a quality source of fiber as well as a great source of other nutrients and phytonutrients. Brown rice is lightly processed (removing only the outermost layer—the hull), allowing it to retain high levels of vitamin B3, B1, B6, manganese, and phosphorus. Studies have shown that brown rice contains "bound" antioxidants that are released by intestinal bacteria, as opposed to antioxidants in fruit which are considered "free" and quickly absorbed into the blood stream. Science has also shown the phytonutrients found in brown rice protect against heart disease and cancer.

Cabbage Cabbage provides vitamin C, which helps to strengthen the immune system. There is also vitamin B, which boosts the metabolism and helps to maintain nerves. Vitamin A benefits skin and eyes, and contains phytonutrients that aid in the production of enzymes that detoxify the liver. Cabbage also provides iodine.

Carrots Carrots contain an abundant amount of vitamins and minerals including vitamin A, C, B1 and B2, magnesium, folate, zinc, copper, and selenium. Various studies have shown that beta-carotene helps reduce cancer risk. Studies have also found that carrots improve heart health and reduce the risk of a coronary event. Studies have confirmed that carrots are good for vision (that's not just an old wives' tale).

Cauliflower Cauliflower provides vitamin C and vitamin K. It also provides minerals to the diet including selenium, iron, zinc, and copper. Cauliflower contains the phytonutrients sulforaphane and isothiocyanate, which help the liver detoxify. It is another source of quality fiber.

Celery Celery will add vitamin C and vitamin K to your pet's diet. Celery contains phthalates that relax the muscles surrounding the arteries. This allows the arteries to dilate and the blood to flow easily. Celery contains many phytochemicals that science has shown prevent abnormal cell growth. Celery also contains a variety of minerals.

Collard Greens This leafy vegetable protects the body against cancer risk due to 'glucosinolates' found in the greens that help support the body's detox and anti-inflammatory systems. This food is a rich source of vitamin K and a good source of vitamin A, C, manganese, and fiber. Do not overcook. Overcooked collard greens emit an unpleasant sulfur smell. Steam for no more than five minutes.

Green Beans Green beans are rich in B vitamins, are shown to have impressive antioxidant qualities, and are a good source of beta-carotenes (just like carrots). Green beans have recently been shown to provide a good source of absorbable silicon (mineral silicon), which is important for bone health and healthy connective tissues.

Mushrooms Mushrooms are a rich source of B-complex vitamins, vitamin D, A, and C. Animal studies have shown that mushrooms help fight cancerous tumors and also serve as a cancer preventive.

Parsley Parsley doesn't just look good on a plate; it has valuable health benefits as well. Parsley contains 'volatile oil' which animal studies have shown help inhibit tumor formation. Parsley also contains flavonoids shown to function as antioxidants, helping to prevent oxygen-based damage to cells. Animal studies have shown that parsley also helps increase the antioxidant capacity of the blood.

Peas Peas contain an assortment of health-protective phytonutrients that have high anti-inflammatory properties and help to prevent cancer, according to studies. One phytonutrient, saponin, is almost exclusively found in peas. It is thought to lower the risk of type II diabetes in humans. Peas provide a quality source of healthy omega-3 fats and vitamin E.

Pumpkin Pumpkin is a high fiber food that provides the body with a good source of the antioxidant beta-carotene. It is a low-calorie and non-meat food that even some of the pickiest cats will consume. This squash also contains one of the highest levels of vitamin A, a natural antioxidant that is essential for good vision and helps protect against lung and mouth cancers. As a natural fiber source, pumpkin helps regulate the intestines and keeps them in good working order. This means that if your pet has a problem with constipation or diarrhea, pumpkin will help the stool get back to a normal consistency. Pumpkin is also an excellent source of carotenes and B-complex vitamins.

Quinoa The Food and Agricultural Organization of the United Nations has declared quinoa as a food with "high nutritive value." Research has shown this food to contain concentrated amounts of beneficial flavonoids that protect cells and help prevent inflammation in the body. Quinoa is a good source of manganese, copper, magnesium, and fiber.

Red/Green Peppers Regardless of color, peppers are an excellent source of vitamins C and A. Peppers also contain vitamin B6 and folic acid, important for reducing levels of homocysteine. High homocysteine levels have been shown to cause damage to blood vessels.

Spinach Spinach is full of vitamins and minerals, containing numerous phytonutrients and at least fourteen different flavonoids. Various studies have shown that eating spinach can reduce cancer risk and also leads to the reduction of the cell division of cancer cells. Spinach is high in vitamin C and A, both of which are natural antioxidants that protect your pet from free radicals. Spinach is high in vitamin K and an excellent source of folate and magnesium.

Sweet Potato Sweet potatoes provide vitamin A and are a tremendous source of beta-carotene. Sweet potatoes have important antioxidant properties and anti-inflammatory properties.

Tomato Tomatoes provide lycopene, an antioxidant that helps to prevent cancerous cell formations. The red coloration of tomatoes is derived from lycopene. Equally nutritious in any form (cooked or raw), unlike most fruits and vegetables, tomatoes actually increase in lycopene when cooked.

Water Chestnuts Water chestnuts are an excellent source of potassium and fiber, and are known to contain detoxifying properties.

Yellow Squash and Zucchini Research studies have found summer squash varieties (yellow, zucchini) to be excellent sources of alpha and beta-carotene (antioxidants). Summer squash is a great source of copper, manganese, vitamin C, and magnesium. Research has also found that steaming this vegetable is the best way to cook it for optimal nutrient retention.

PASTA AND DAIRY

Cheese Cheese provides protein and a quality source of calcium. Cheese also provides iron, zinc and potassium.

Whole Wheat Pasta Whole wheat is the health benefit to this pasta. Whole wheat provides your pet with a quality fiber source and is also a good source of nutrients such as manganese and magnesium.

Yogurt Most yogurt provides your pet with friendly bacteria or probiotics. The bacteria promotes healthy intestines and a strong immune system. Yogurt provides multiple vitamins and also a nice source of calcium for your pet. Plain, low-fat yogurt is a healthy option.

SUPPLEMENTS

Calcium Supplement or Eggshells Calcium aids in maintaining bone and teeth health. Studies have shown that calcium prevents some types of cancer and reduces obesity. Human studies have shown an increase of bone mass density and a reduction of arthritis pain from the use of eggshell calcium.

Coconut oil Studies have shown that consuming coconut oil can help humans resist viruses and bacteria that cause illness. Coconut oil also contains medium chain triglyceride fats, which have been shown to aid the liver in the efficient burning of energy. While little to no research proves that the consumption of coconut oil would provide the same benefit to pets, most research for human health is performed on animals. We can safely assume that our pets will receive the same health benefits from coconut oil that we do.

Cod Liver Oil Cod liver oil provides vitamin A, which helps maintain a strong immune system, and vitamin D, which maintains strong and healthy bones. Cod liver oil is a great source of healthy omega-3 fatty acids. This oil contains EPA (Eicosa Pentaenoic Acid), good for the cardiovascular system in helping to reduce inflammation in the body, and DHA (Docosa Hexaenoic Acid), which is good for eyesight, skin, and a healthy nervous system.

Olive Oil Pure, extra virgin olive oil is one of the most beneficial types of oils for consumption. It is rich in monounsaturated fat. Recent studies have shown that olive oil may cut the risk of coronary heart disease in half in humans, and it has also been shown to have very potent antioxidant effects.

Sunflower Seeds Sunflower seeds are an excellent source of vitamin E and a good source of B1, manganese, magnesium, copper, selenium, phosphorus, and folate. Sunflower seeds are high in vitamin E, which have antioxidants that help neutralize free radicals that could otherwise damage cells. Studies found that sunflower seeds were one of several seeds and nuts that contained phytosterol. Phytosterols are believed to reduce blood levels of cholesterol, enhance the immune system, and decrease the risk of cancer. Sunflower seeds are also a good source of magnesium, which is necessary for bone health and energy production.

HEALTH CONDITIONS CURED BY NUTRITION

Naïvely, when Susan and I first wrote *Dinner PAWsible*, we thought the majority of our target audience would be buying the cookbook to feed their healthy pets. What we realized through many conversations with pet owners is that people don't look for alternatives to commercial food until there is some kind of a problem with their dog's or cat's health.

As an integrative veterinarian, I've really learned that this is the case! It's not until my clients' pets experience health issues that they are willing to change from the convenience of kibble in a bag to making their own food for their pets. I commonly cite that 80% of the health conditions that walk through the door at my clinic can be cured with food. The great news is that there are some health conditions that can be exclusively treated with nutrition. Examples include diabetes in cats and irritable bowel syndrome in both dogs and cats; other conditions depend on the cause and the patient. For some patients with seizures or recurrent ear infections, I can treat them exclusively with food; other patients need a little bit more work than that. However, these examples should give you hope as you buy and use this cookbook. Know that there are many conditions that you can treat at home through great nutrition rather than expensive medication.

I would like to share three case histories with you to show that, in the right circumstances, all it takes is good food to cure the following health conditions: **diabetes**, **pancreatitis**, and **chronic ear infections**.

Our first example is the story of Chewbacca, a six-year-old domestic long-haired tabby cat. Chewy is a big boy! When he first became sick and was diagnosed with **diabetes**, he weighed twenty-two pounds. His proper body weight should have been fifteen or sixteen pounds. To put this in perspective, it would be like a human weighing 230 pounds when he should actually weigh 150. It's a big weight difference and it causes a lot of damage to the joints, heart, and many internal organs. When a diet is predominantly based on carbohydrates, it also seriously damages the insulin-producing cells of the pancreas. Because most commonly purchased grocery store foods and veterinary prescription diets are based on carbohydrates, it is very easy for our domestic cats to become grossly overweight. Just like humans who eat too many carbohydrates and are overweight, all of a sudden these overweight cats can become very ill. Signs of diabetes include excessive drinking of water, urination, bladder infections, and rapid weight loss. What I'm describing is called type II diabetes in humans, and it is the type of diabetes that affects most overweight adult cats. The illness comes about when the body consumes too many carbohydrates, which really is another word for sugars, until the pancreas cannot make enough insulin to put all that sugar into storage. Essentially, the pancreas burns out. A body that cannot regulate its sugar does not maintain good energy and becomes ill. Insulin is the treatment for type I diabetes, the so-called juvenile onset of diabetes in humans. It is also the type of diabetes dogs get. However, insulin does very little to regulate type II diabetes in an overweight cat. In spite of the ineffectiveness of insulin in cats, insulin is still used as a common treatment by many veterinarians.

So, when these cats go to the vet for follow-up blood glucose checks, their glucose level is still quite high.

This is what was going on with Chewbacca when I was first introduced to him. Chewy was on a veterinary-prescribed diabetes diet that consisted of dry kibble. In fact, dry kibble comprises a minimum of 30% carbohydrates, which gives it its crunchy texture. This meant that Chewy's original owner was inadvertently doing nothing to control his blood sugar levels. His food was also left out all day so he could snack whenever he wanted. When Chewy went to a new home, his new caretaker was more aware of the importance of nutrition and started offering him the Turkey & Salmon Hash cat food recipe from this cookbook (pg 97). Chewbacca communicated clearly that this was his favorite recipe, and no longer ate crunchy kibble.

Chewbacca, photo courtesy of Nancy Wajda

Chewy quickly lost two pounds and his blood sugar went from 438 to 110 (a normal blood sugar range is 80–120). Chewbacca does still have some ways to go to lose his excess weight, and his new diet will get him to his goal.

Pancreatitis is another illness that is often treated just by good nutrition. When a dog with pancreatitis is hospitalized, typical treatment includes IV fluids and nothing by the mouth for the next few days—no food, no water, absolutely nothing! The pancreas has two jobs: the first is sugar regulation, as in the case of Chewy and his diabetes, and the second job relates to digestion. In pancreatitis, the enzymes that are produced in the pancreas, which are normally kept inactive until they reach the intestines, become active in the pancreas and start digestion in the pancreas itself, instead of the intestines. This can be very painful. The patient has to wait for his pancreas to calm down and thus cannot consume anything during the recovery period. Once it's time for the sick pet to start eating again, the selection of food is very important.

Madonna is a gorgeous little three-pound Yorkshire terrier whom I met when she was experiencing recurrent cases of pancreatitis. Previous veterinarians had put her on a prescription diet meant to decrease the risk of pancreatitis. However, this diet did not work for Madonna, because it contained rice. Dogs do not have a lot of a specific pancreatic enzyme called amylase, which digests rice and other carbohydrates.

When I met little Madonna we started with the usual IV fluids and a few days without eating anything so her pancreas and intestines could have a rest. She stopped vomiting and her bloody, mucus-like diarrhea stopped as well. When it was time to start eating again, we started slowly with foods that are easy for a dog to digest. For dogs, this is delicious chicken broth with no additives that has been homemade in the kitchen. For the first twenty-four hours, Madonna drank only chicken broth. On day two, her mother made fresh broth and included some vegetables in it, such as little pieces of carrots and green beans. Madonna ate that very well. By the third day, we were including small pieces of chicken meat. Now, Madonna is very well regulated and hasn't had any flare-ups of pancreatitis in years, when she used to have them every couple

Madonna

of months. Her snacks are a piece of Romaine lettuce. She also shares plain yogurt with her mother at lunchtime and eats berries when they are freshly in season. As long as her mother makes her fresh meats and vegetables, Madonna does great.

Pancreatitis can be life threatening, especially if it goes on undetected for years.

Fortunately, ear infections aren't life threatening, but they can certainly make a dog and her family miserable. **Chronic ear infections** are another health issue that can be prevented through a great diet. Obviously, when a dog comes in and is in the middle of a nasty ear infection, medication needs to be used to treat the presentation. But we don't want our dog to suffer and continue to experience recurring infections; we want to get to the underlying cause. More often than not, dogs are just treated for their symptoms and the root cause is never addressed. And in recurrent ear infections, a food allergy is the cause 95% of the time.

For some dogs, it's as simple as removing grains from their diets to take care of ear infections. For others, it's not that easy to identify the cause of the allergy. For little Bentley, a gorgeous Maltese, it was a little bit more difficult than just taking out grains. Bentley is allergic to most meat proteins and many vegetables. When most allergies start, it's usually attributed to only one or two things. However if they continue, they can grow to cover multiple foods. It is possible that Bentley started out allergic to chicken, and, as he tried different foods with many different ingredients, he became allergic to more and more things like beef, oats, barley, sweet potato, lamb, peanut butter, and so on. The only foods Bentley can eat to control his allergies are tuna and brussel sprouts! How is that for a tasty combination? Now that we have removed all the foods that make our little man itch, he has been comfortable for almost two years. He no longer has ear infections and does not chew the fur out of his belly anymore. Now, obviously tuna and brussel sprouts are not a completely balanced diet, and Bentley is on some supplements that help finish out the balance in his meals. But his mother is so happy that her little man doesn't keep both of them awake all night scratching and rubbing his ears.

These stories are just examples of how I have used nutrition in my veterinary practice to cure my patients. All of the conditions listed in the subsequent section have been treated successfully in my office with nutrition. For some, great food is enough, for others, it requires additional herbs, medicines, or some other kind of treatment.

WHAT TO FEED FOR SPECIFIC HEALTH ISSUES

Since we first shared these recipes with pet parents, thousands of pets are enjoying our healthy meals. At the same time, we have also been asked regular questions about what kinds of food are good for specific health conditions. Our cookbook was originally written with the healthy patient in mind; however, owners whose pets have an illness are frequently looking for recipes to restore their pets' health. This chapter is written as a guideline for all those pet owners. Most of the time, the recipes here already provide what you would need for many health conditions. However, let's discuss some specific diagnoses.

Seniors

Older pets can have multiple health conditions or simply be suffering the maladies of aging. For the dog or cat who is getting old, natural physical changes include a graying muzzle and a little less energy; or it can also mean arthritis, kidney disease, bladder infection, cancer, liver disease, heart disease, and many other serious health problems. Specific conditions will be addressed below. Commercial senior foods often add glucosamine and/or chondroitin for joint health, and omega fatty acids for coat and anti-inflammatory effects. In dry kibble, these ingredients are rarely present in a high enough concentration to have an effect on the aged patient.

Omega fatty acids can be provided by consuming cod liver oil—a staple in the recipes in this book. Flax seed, hemp, and mixed nut oils can also be used in the diet to provide anti-inflammatory effects needed by geriatric patients. Cartilage soup instead of bone broth can also be helpful for achy joints in dogs (pg 202).

Kidney

There are two philosophies on how to deal with kidney failure. The philosophy of the pet food industry is to feed the patient low protein food. They claim that less protein is lost by the challenged kidneys on low protein diets. This is true—less in equals less out. However, ask yourself what makes up muscle. The answer is protein. If you feed your pet a low protein diet, the kidney failure patient will lose muscle, making the pet weak.

The whole food concept for the renal failure patient is to feed high quality proteins (real meat), so the failing kidneys can retain as much quality protein as possible More protein eaten provides more building blocks for muscle health, giving the kidney patient more strength for everyday life. The result is a better quality of life. Kidney patients should be fed balanced meals like the ones in this book. Plus, there is more naturally occurring liquid in a real food diet, which means more fluids to nourish the kidneys—another bonus for kidneys that leak out too much water.

Bladder

Bladder problems consist of infection and stones. In most cases, the key to good bladder health is the right urine pH; the urine should be acidic. Meat protein is the best way to produce acidic urine. Most commercial diets treat bladder conditions using chemicals that make urine more acidic, rather than simply using meat protein. Because meats are the main protein source in the recipes in this book, our recipes will help dogs and cats with bladder health issues. Regardless of the type of crystals or stones that your dog or cat has, a well-balanced diet with lots of moisture creates normal urine pH (6.5–7), resulting in optimal bladder health. As with any patient with a health issue, monitoring will help early detection and prevention. We recommend that patients who've had bladder troubles get routine urinalysis to make sure any potential issues are identified early.

Struvite crystals and stones are the most common bladder stone in both dogs and cats. Struvites start with a bladder infection. Then, salt normally found in the urine forms crystals around the bacteria. These crystals get bigger and bigger as time goes on, and become stones. Struvites can be prevented by stopping bladder infections from starting. Feeding your pets a meat diet will produce acidic urine and help prevent infections.

Calcium oxalate stones are the second most common type of bladder stone in dogs, and they are also diet related. Foods to avoid include: peanut butter, sesame seeds, lentils, potatoes, sweet potatoes, and spinach. Low oxalate foods include: beef, eggs, cheese, fish, pasta, broccoli, turnips, melons, peaches, and wild rice. Also, substitute turnips for whole wheat pasta. Replace the liver with eggs (hard-boiled or scrambled). Replace mushrooms with shrimp. Low oxalate recipes in this book which don't need modifications include: Turkey and Oats (pg 140), Turkey Meatloaf (pgs 96 & 142), Meatloaf (pg 155), Mutt Burger (pg 163), Scrambled Eggs & Fruit (pg 168). However, simple modifications make most recipes safe for the oxalate-prone patient.

Urate crystals are a genetic issue for a few dog breeds, especially dalmatians and bulldogs. Some cats get urate crystals too. Formation of urate crystals/stones relates to the poor breakdown of protein because of a liver that doesn't work normally. Foods to avoid include organ meats, anchovies, mackerel, and sardines. To prevent urates, diets also need to be low in fat because fatty foods grab onto protein and make urate-prone dogs more likely to form urate stones. Recipes that don't need modifications include: Turkey and Oats (pg 140), Turkey and Salmon Hash (pgs 97 & 141), Turkey Meatloaf (pgs 96 & 142), Beef Stew (pg 154), Meatloaf (pg 155), Chili (pg 162), Mutt Burger (pg 163), Scrambled Eggs & Fruit (pg 168), Scrambled Eggs, Bacon & Sweet Potato Hash Browns (pg 166), and the Liver Detoxification Diet (pg 204).

Silicate crystals most likely form when dogs have acidic urine and eat a lot of corn gluten and/or soybean hulls. Read the label of most inexpensive, well-advertised commercial pet foods and you will find these ingredients listed. In addition, commercial diets meant for bladder health can still be full of these problem-causing by-products. The good news is that these ingredients are easy to avoid with a real food diet. Any *Dinner PAWsible* recipe would be appropriate for these patients.

Cystine crystals and stones are another example of a genetically inherited health issue for some dogs. Cysteine is another breakdown product of protein, thus the conventional theory is to feed the dog less protein. A healthier alternative is a diet with moderate amounts of high-quality protein. Routine monitoring will also help these dogs. Any of the recipes in this book that use under 35 g protein would be appropriate, as long as the protein is of high quality and holds a lot of moisture to flush out the system.

Calcium phosphate stones form when there is not enough acid in the urine. The natural way to add acid to the urine is to feed your pet a meat-based diet. These *Dinner PAWsible* recipes will do that. Dog and cat patients whose urines still have a high pH level (meaning that there is not enough acid, since low pH values are acidic) even after a change in diet are probably suffering from other health issues like a systemic yeast infection.

Pancreas

This very important organ has two functions: sugar regulation and digestion. Common problems and illnesses associated with the pancreas include diabetes and pancreatitis.

Diabetes in cats is almost exclusively treated with diet. Studies and real-life cases show that diabetic cats have little to no reduction in their blood sugar levels with insulin administration. Diabetic cats are just like type II diabetic humans—if they get the extra weight off and stop eating carbohydrates, many will get better on their own. Some cats have other health issues alongside diabetes, which means that treatment will not be as straightforward. However, removing carbohydrates from a cat's diet will take care of many of these issues. Most of our recipes for cats are grain-free, except Gumbo (pgs 119 & 173), Chicken and Rice Casserole (pgs 122 & 182), and Chicken Scallopini (pgs 128 & 188).

Diabetes in dogs is just like type I diabetes in humans. This is an autoimmune disease where the immune system attacks the pancreas, the organ that produces insulin. As in the case of humans, diet plays a role; however insulin is a medical necessity for this type of diabetes. A low-carbohydrate diet will help diabetic dogs manage their disease, but it should not be the sole treatment, as it is for cats. Diabetic dogs will need to eat the grain-free recipes in *Dinner PAWsible*, which can be found in a special grain-free chapter (pg 193). Modifications to other regular recipes can also produce grain-free meals. To do so, replace brown rice with quinoa and whole-wheat pasta with chard, collard greens, kale, or other leafy greens. A great diabetic snack is a slice of bitter melon—a fruit that naturally reduces blood sugar.

Pancreatitis is the other common pancreatic illness. The pancreas makes many of the digestive enzymes that the body needs. These enzymes have handles on them that keep the enzymes inactive until they are secreted into the intestines. In pancreatitis, the handles come off the enzymes while they are still in the pancreas; the result is that the pancreas starts to be digested. This is painful and leads to infection. Treatment for pancreatitis is hospitalization, fluids, and rest. But afterwards, the goal is to prevent recurrence of the condition. While causes of pancreatitis are not known, high fat meals and high carbohydrate diets are related to pancreatic disease. Therefore, unprocessed diets of real food are great preventive medicine. Many of these dogs do well on a grain-free diet (grain-free recipes for dogs can be found on page 193). Modifications to other regular recipes can produce grain-free meals. Replace brown rice with quinoa and replace whole wheat pasta with chard, collard greens, kale, or other leafy greens.

Cancer

Cancer is inflammation gone wrong. When a pet is diagnosed with cancer, along with treating the cancer we must also address the inflammation in the body by feeding the sick pet foods that are the least inflammatory. The ultimate anti-inflammatory diet for cancer patients is raw meat and puréed vegetables, including mushrooms and turmeric. Don't worry if you are uncomfortable with feeding your pet raw or lightly cooked meat. As long as you prepare their food at home, you are still light-years away from the owner who feeds them dry kibble and processed foods, which are pro-inflammatory. Any recipe in this book can be made with raw meat. Follow the same grain-free guidelines as previously stated: In regular recipes, replace brown rice with quinoa and replace whole wheat pasta with chard, collard greens, kale, or other leafy greens.

Allergies

Allergies commonly come in three forms: food, flea, and hay fever. If you control your pets' fleas and feed them great food, then the risk of hay fever will be lessened. If you suspect that your dog has food allergies (chronic ear infections are a signal), it can be difficult to figure out which particular food is the cause. The first place to begin is to go grain-free. This includes treats. After three weeks on a grain-free diet, if your pet is still showing signs of food allergies, work with your veterinarian to get to the bottom line. It could be anything—any meat, any vegetable, *anything* (I have even had a patient allergic to apple cider vinegar)! The problem may really be that the pet's liver needs to be detoxified, or that he or she is allergic to something else weird and uncommon, like plug-in air fresheners. An allergy elimination trial, muscle testing, or food allergy testing using a saliva-based test can assist in finding the culprit.

Liver

The liver is responsible for many detoxification pathways in the body. When the body has been exposed to too many toxins, or there is a genetic predisposition (little dogs with red tear stains under their eyes), the liver can no longer detoxify the body and it becomes ill. A great liver detoxification diet was developed by an amazing veterinary colleague, Dr. Jean Dodds, who developed the diet according to foods that have shown to be the least stressful for the liver according to her research (page 204). Feed this diet to the patient for two to four weeks for a short cleanse, or long-term if the liver has permanent damage. Epileptic patients on phenobarbital are a good example of those who need long-term liver detoxification. For those on an intermittent cleanse, the recipes in *Dinner PAWsible* are great as they use very few processed ingredients.

Sensitive stomach

Sensitive tummies may be fixed as easily as taking away processed foods and feeding your pets a balanced diet of real food, just like the recipes in this cookbook. Sometimes, noticing what food substance comes back up in vomit or is undigested in the feces can help you identify the problem. Dealing with the problem is possibly as easy as removing that food from the diet. Carrots are an example of one food that commonly comes back up and, once removed, fixes the sensitive stomach issue.

Sensitive stomach patients can be broken up into the groups that vomit, those who only have diarrhea, those who experience both vomiting and diarrhea, those with constipation, and those who regurgitate their food. Regurgitation—when the food looks exactly like it was before consumed except for a little extra fluid—is usually a chiropractic issue. Sometimes regurgitation happens when the food is eaten too fast or when it does not agree with the animal's stomach. The other symptoms of sensitive stomach are discussed below.

Vomiting and diarrhea: As long as your dog is an adult and fully vaccinated against parvovirus, the proper home treatment for vomiting is nothing by mouth for twenty-four hours—and I mean nothing, not even water! If your dog continues to vomit, or has blood in the vomit, then this is a medical emergency. On the other hand, if your dog is one of those with a sensitive tummy and experiences vomiting issues frequently, no food for twenty-four hours is the proper treatment. Again, not a thing by mouth, including water, for twenty-four hours after the last vomit. In contrast, vomiting in cats is a medical emergency.

After twenty-four hours, if your dog has stopped vomiting, slowly reintroduce liquids. Water is good in small amounts—a ⅛–¼ cup every hour until your dog no longer guzzles the water down. Even better for rehydration is bone broth (see recipe on page 205).

After twenty-four hours of just liquids, it is time to reintroduce food. The standard recommendation for an upset stomach is boiled hamburger and rice. Before jumping to this meal, let's first look briefly at the canine digestive system. Unlike humans, dogs have a lot less amylase, a digestive enzyme necessary to break down rice. As a result, you should not feed rice to soothe the upset stomach of a hungry dog. Instead, think about what a dog is meant to eat—meat. If your dog has been vomiting and you have corrected the vomiting, start by feeding small amounts of meats. Then, slowly add vegetables and, if your dog is not on a grain-free diet, is it time to reintroduce rice or pasta after a couple of days.

Diarrhea (without vomiting) is well managed by adding pumpkin to the food. Plain old canned pumpkin—not pumpkin pie mix—that is either home canned or store bought. Pumpkin does a great job of regulating the intestines.

Constipation is treated in the same way as diarrhea—with pumpkin. Both dogs and cats will eat pumpkin, which has good intestinal benefits.

Inflammatory bowel syndrome/ disease (IBD)

Many IBD patients need grain-free options. Some IBD patients struggle with the disease their whole lives, and this condition can be difficult to treat. A grain-free approach is the first place to start (grain-free recipes can be found on page 193). Modifications to other regular recipes can produce grain-free meals. Replace brown rice with quinoa and replace whole wheat pasta with sweet potatoes or leafy vegetables.

Poor coat

Whether it is shedding, dandruff, or a greasy coat, a poor hair coat is the first signal of inflammation in dogs and cats. If we feed a high quality home-cooked diet, many of the poor coat issues will resolve. High quality ingredients, like those in our recipes, will go a long way to address coat issues. For the dog with a very greasy coat, yeast infection may be the cause, and it may be best to feed him a grain-free diet (grain-free recipes can be found page 193). Modifications to other regular recipes can produce grain-free meals. Replace brown rice with quinoa and replace whole wheat pasta with sweet potatoes or leafy vegetables. Some of these yeasty dogs do well with a yeast cleanse—a product that can be obtained from a holistic veterinarian.

Pregnancy and lactation

Pregnancy demands extra calories and extra calcium. Dogs and cats are pregnant for about sixty-three days. In the last trimester, which lasts three to four weeks (when their bellies get big and the pregnancy starts to show), pregnant dogs and cats should be fed twice the normal amount of calories and twice the amount of daily calcium. Once the puppies and kittens are born, the same rule applies for the first month—double the calories and calcium for mom—until the babies start eating on their own. For really large litters, even more food for mom may be needed. Watch her hips; if they start getting bony, she needs more food.

Puppies and kittens

Just as the mothers need double the calories and calcium during pregnancy and breastfeeding, puppies and kittens need increased calories and calcium for growth.

Kittens eat twice what adult cats eat until they are twelve to eighteen months old. Therefore, they should be fed double the portion of a similarly sized adult and double the calcium.

Puppy diets take a little more work to figure out as amounts to be fed depend on the breed. The larger the breed, the more calcium the puppy needs. Small breed dogs will do well with doubled calories and calcium as listed in our recipes. On the other hand, giant breed dogs, like mastiffs, need massive amounts of calcium to keep up with their growth. These dogs will do very well growing on the *Dinner PAWsible* recipes, but please work with your veterinarian to make sure you are providing enough calcium as the pup grows, since the required quantity of calcium changes with every ten to fifteen pounds of weight gained. Not enough calcium can lead to bone pain, and even deformity if the deficiency is large enough. Similarly, too much calcium can lead to growing too fast. Therefore, if you have a large breed puppy, it is important to work with a holistic veterinarian when trying to decide the correct amount of calcium in the diet.

Heart disease (congestive heart failure—CHF)

As is the case in humans, diet can help greatly to manage the symptoms of CHF. Commercial diets are often high in salt, which worsens the symptoms of heart failure, raising blood pressure. Therefore, the best way to deal with pets with heart disease is to prepare their food at home. Balanced home-cooked foods that are fed in rotation as we suggest will help heart patients have a better quality of life, and they will live longer too. Some patients on blood pressure medication will find a dramatic decrease in blood pressure simply by removing added salt from the diet. When available, using heart as the organ meat in recipes, sometimes replacing liver, is a healthy addition. A sprinkle of hawthorne berry on the food from time to time is another topping that is healthy for the heart.

Intervertebral disc disease—IVDD

These patients need everything anti-inflammatory. Therefore, do not feed them commercial foods, especially not the foods that contain dyes, grains, and by-products. Grain-free real foods are best, simply because there is less inflammation associated with grain-free foods. For the recipes that use rice or pasta, substitute in sweet potato or even quinoa in equal amounts. Because IVDD is painful and can cause permanent damage to the spine, preventing future occurrences is best. Great food coupled with routine chiropractic (veterinary spinal manipulation therapy), herbal, and acupuncture therapy can really help the disc patient have a great quality of life. The collagen in chicken foot soup (pg 202) can help as well.

Joints

Many commercial foods say that they contain a 'natural' source of glucosamine. Sadly, much of the time this natural glucosamine comes from fermented corn, which is not a reliable source for joint supplements. Additionally, there is often not enough nutraceutical (glucosamine and/or chondroitin) in food to make a difference. A healthier way to lubricate joints through food is to feed cartilage soup as discussed previously for seniors. Another fun food additive: When preparing eggshell calcium, rather than throwing out the eggshell lining (the thin film surrounding the inside of the egg), include it in the food. Eggshell lining is an ingredient in some joint supplements.

Eyes

There are two broad issues involving the eyes: tear staining and loss of sight. Loss of sight is best addressed through avoidance and prevention by feeding the best quality foods, that is human foods that are balanced and varied as we have suggested. Some vision issues, like cataracts, can be genetically driven. However, introducing a great diet from the beginning can slow the progression of cataracts. Tear staining, especially red tears, brings us back to the liver function as discussed previously. Many dogs with red tear staining show significant improvement with the liver detoxification diet.

Seizures

Seizures are debilitating and it is often hard to find the root cause. It is difficult to stop seizures, even with medicine. For some seizure patients, it is as simple as removing processed foods from their diet and the seizures should stop. For others, it may mean no grains as well. Some may benefit from a liver detoxification diet. And still for others, all of these things may reduce the frequency or severity of the seizures but may not stop them. However, all seizure patients can benefit from liver detoxification and great nutrition.

Anal glands

Four to five different things can cause repeated anal gland issues: dogs with docked tails, patients needing chiropractic therapy, a low fiber diet, yeast infection, and whole body inflammation. While the first two conditions can't be corrected with diet, the last three can. Carbohydrates in the diet feed yeast into the body, therefore the carbohydrates in processed foods create inflammation through that yeast. The recipes in this book will provide your pet with enough fiber to stimulate emptying of the anal glands and reduce inflammation. Grain-free recipes will slow the growth of yeast. Use either the recipes in the grain-free chapter (pg 193) or substitute brown rice and whole wheat pasta with sweet potatoes, quinoa, or green leafy vegetables.

Overweight animals

Diets that are high in carbohydrates will cause weight gain (that, plus a sedentary lifestyle). The crazy thing is that most commercial weight control diets are high in carbohydrates (often called fiber). Inadvertently, senior and weight control diets can actually lead to weight gain. Instead, feed balanced and low-carbohydrate real food diets to your pet as described in this cookbook. For more rapid weight loss, feed grain-free recipes as grains are often the source of carbohydrates in many diets. Fortunately, simply making a change from commercial to real food will cause most dogs and cats to lose weight. We are also trained by pet food companies to think that cats graze all day. Dry cat food in the bowl is like chocolate chip cookies in the jar—whenever we walk by we will sneak in a snack every time, leading to weight gain. Just as we feed ourselves and our dogs with regular meals twice a day, we should feed our cats in the same way. The hardest part will be listening to the cat complaining for a week as it gets used to not being able to snack at will.

FREQUENTLY ASKED QUESTIONS

Where do I start?

I always start with stew—I find it's really easy. After that, start branching out with more recipes.

How do I transition my dog to home-cooked food?

If your dog has an iron gut, go ahead and make the switch. But, many dogs are very sensitive. For these dogs, ease them into the diet slowly. Take a week or two to switch from commercial food to home-prepared foods.

How do I transition my cat to home-cooked food?

Cats are cats. Some cats will take quite a long time to switch over; others are ready at the first meal. If your cat is the skeptical sort, be patient. Offer tiny amounts of food once or twice a day. Don't let the food stay out for long—cats don't like the smell of spoiled food. One of my cats took a year to switch.

Can I go back to kibble or canned commercial food if I'm traveling or don't have home-prepared food ready?

Yes. Some pets do just fine with these changes. However, some pets will have an upset tummy if you abruptly switch them back to commercial food (or change their diet in any fashion). Imagine eating healthy food for weeks then pigging out on donuts and high energy drinks; you'd have a stomach ache too. Try it out at home first instead of finding out the hard way on a trip.

Will my pets lose weight when I switch from commercial to home-prepared?

Overweight pets do lose weight if fed these home-prepared recipes simply because their carbohydrate intake is drastically reduced. Pets who are at their ideal weight are less likely to have weight loss issues. In fact, finicky pets who are a bit thin often gain weight as they will come to really like their new homemade meals for the first time in their lives. If your dog does not lose weight, he or she may have a thyroid issue and should be tested by a veterinarian.

How much do I feed my pet?

If you are currently feeding them high quality kibble, start with the same volume of food when you switch to these recipes. After two weeks, check your pet's weight. Some animals lose weight while some will gain it since different metabolisms respond differently to high quality food. Adjust the portions as needed. Regardless of your dog's or cat's metabolism, you are doing a good thing by switching to human-grade food.

My pet needs to lose weight. How do I adjust these recipes?

Feed for the weight you want your dog or cat to be. If your dog should weigh forty-five pounds, then feed as if your dog is forty-five pounds. If you feed for the sixty pounds your dog is, no change will occur!

What if my pet gets too thin?

Some dogs and cats need a few more calories, just like there are some humans who need to gain weight. This is a bigger problem for dogs on a grain-free diet as grains provide the calories. If you are feeding your dog a grain-free diet and he or she has lost too much weight, add in sweet potato or beans. If your dog is not allergic to grain, whole wheat pasta or brown rice are good sources of calories to help your dog maintain an ideal weight.

However, do be aware that there are health issues that can cause weight loss. Be sure to keep your holistically minded veterinarian in the loop when working with weight loss issues. Diabetes, kidney failure, hyperthyroidism in cats, and even cancer can cause unexplained weight loss.

Can I make these recipes in a slow cooker?

Most definitely! The goal is to make your life and your pet's life better, not increase your workload. If you prepare recipes in bulk (pg 44 on how to make large batches), everything can be put straight into the slow cooker and cooked on low for twelve hours. One factor will be the size of your slow cooker—most are four or seven quarts in size.

Can I feed my pet milk?

This answer depends on your pet. Some animals have always had milk and do fine; others will develop frightening diarrhea. Try offering a small amount once. Wait a day and see what happens. If there is a bit of diarrhea, skip the milk. Yogurt and cheese in small amounts may still be OK. Again, try a small amount and wait a day to see. A great type of milk to try is raw goat's milk—it is easier to digest and has wonderful healing properties.

What about raw foods?

This is a question of great debate. Some pet parents insist on raw because that was how animals ate in the wild. My training and my pets have taught me that some pets just can't do raw, for example older animals or the sick patient. Dogs and cats who are always cold (the ones that love to sleep in the sun or under a blanket) tend not to do well with raw food either. Some people just can't stand the idea of feeding their pets raw meat. That's OK. Do what's comfortable. If you are comfortable with raw meats, remember to handle the food properly. Even if you feed raw meat, you'll still want to steam the vegetables.

What about supplements?

Our idea was to create recipes that were well balanced so the pet owner wouldn't have to deal with supplements; there is so much confusing information out there! The key is variety in the diet. If you make the same recipe day after day and meal after meal, your pet's diet won't be balanced, in which case you would need a supplement. The most common supplements needed are calcium and a general vitamin (there should be no iron in the vitamin). Personally, I like Animal Essentials Seaweed Calcium and Standard Process Catalyn vitamins, which you can find online or with your holistic veterinarian.

Is it ok to season the food?

Seasonings are known to help with digestion. In limited amounts, seasoning the food will help our pets. Many dogs like the flavors seasoning introduces. Cats, well, it all depends on the cat. Don't over-season, and ask your pet if it smells good (put the herb bottle under their nose and make sure they don't turn their head away or sneeze violently).

Can I use garlic in the recipes?

Garlic is a controversial seasoning. Some evidence presented on the internet suggests that garlic is poisonous to dogs and cats. In actuality, when cooked, in small amounts for flavoring, garlic can actually be medicinal, even helping with digestion and flea control.

Can I use onion in the recipes?

Raw onions can be fatal. If you cook with onions, it needs to be a very small amount. For example, if you make a meatloaf which contains a little onion, once cooked, it will be safe to share with your pets. No onion rings please!

Can I feed my pet bones?

Cooked bones splinter and kill, especially chicken and pork bones. Raw bones are usually spongy; however, they may still cause problems. Always think before you give something to your pet. If it's likely to cause problems, don't give it to the animal. Interestingly, bones from canned fish are spongy and can be a good source of calcium; and they have been included in a few recipes in this book.

How about chocolate?

Nope—not safe. Especially not baking chocolate.

Can't I just feed my pet table scraps?

We need to feed the healthy parts of what we do eat, not the parts we don't eat. The fat from the steak is not as healthy as the steak. Lean meat and veggies are really the best way to go. Other things to avoid from the table include starches. Dogs and cats don't have anywhere near the same starch digestion capabilities as humans do. We have salivary amylase to start the breakdown process in our mouths; but they don't. So, keep the breadcrumbs for the birds and feed that last bite of chicken breast as a treat to your pet.

Can I add extra meat and vegetables to these recipes?

If you've got a big eater, you can certainly add more vegetables or fruit to any recipe. If you add more meat you are adding to the protein percentage of the food, which is not necessary nutrition-wise.

I've heard some say that 'people food' isn't good for dogs and cats. Is this true?

Some people food isn't safe for dogs and cats, for example grapes, raisins, and onions. However, most foods are perfectly safe and healthy. Remember, pet food is made from people food (or at least it should be) that has been highly processed and is no longer recognizable. Look at all the advertising for pet food these days —it sure looks like people food to me!

Most commercial pet foods say that they are "100% complete and balanced." Are your *Dinner PAWsible* recipes completely balanced?

No single recipe provides 100% of the daily nutritional needs as recommended by the National Research Council. However, each recipe is close to NRC daily recommendations. My own food isn't balanced at every meal; is yours? By eating a variety of foods over time, our diet becomes balanced. That is what we hope you will do for your pets with these recipes.

Food is not an exact science, not even for commercial food. Many things can alter the nutritional content in food such as growing conditions, freshness of ingredients, cooking time, and temperature. Even commercial foods can change in nutritional content from batch to batch because of many variables. Knowing this, we prefer that pets eat a variety of foods that will ensure that their diets will be balanced over time.

A plate of chicken and sardines for dogs.

CATS

TURKEY FOR CATS

Turkey Dinner

Turkey Meatloaf

Turkey & Salmon Hash

Turkey & Shrimp

♪ TURKEY DINNER

Protein: 19 grams **Fat:** 8 grams **Calories:** 175
Daily serving for a 10 lb cat; can be divided into 2 feedings.

• •

½ cup [125 mL] turkey breast, cooked, skin removed, shredded
   or ground
2 tablespoons [30 mL] chicken hearts cooked, ground fine
1 teaspoon [5 mL] black beans, cooked, fork mashed
1 teaspoon [5 mL] cod liver oil
150 mg calcium from a supplement or slightly less than ⅛ tsp
   finely ground eggshell
¼ cup [60 mL] broth (if desired)

Combine turkey and chicken hearts in medium bowl and mix well.
Add beans, oil, and calcium, and mix. Add broth if desired, and
mix again. Serve.

Hint: Mashed black beans will turn the food a gray color.
Don't worry, it's natural food coloring!

☽ TURKEY MEATLOAF

Protein: 21 grams **Fat:** 13 grams **Calories:** 225
Daily serving for a 10 lb cat; can be divided into 2 feedings.

. . . .

½ cup [125 mL] ground turkey, raw
½ raw egg
1 teaspoon [5 mL] peas, mashed
½ teaspoon [2.5 mL] parsley, fresh ground (optional)
1 teaspoon [5 mL] sunflower seeds, dried, no salt added, ground
    fine
150 mg calcium from a supplement or slightly less than ⅛ tsp
    finely ground eggshell
¼ cup [60 mL] broth (if desired)
1 teaspoon [5 mL] tomato paste, canned

Combine turkey and egg in a medium bowl, and mix well. Add peas, parsley, sunflower seeds, and calcium, and mix. Add 1 tablespoon of bone broth, if desired. Mix well and shape into a loaf. Place in a loaf-sized baking dish. Add tomato paste to top, pour remaining broth (optional) on top. Bake in a 350-degree oven until internal temperature reaches 185°F. Allow to cool and serve.

Hint: Most cats aren't fans of vegetables. Mashing them into your home-cooked meal AND adding homemade broth ensures that your cats receive the nutrients they need.

♪ TURKEY & SALMON HASH

Protein: 26 grams **Fat:** 13 grams **Calories:** 238
Daily serving for a 10 lb cat; can be divided into 2 feedings.

. . . .

½ cup [125 mL] ground turkey, raw
¼ cup [60 mL] salmon, canned, pink, with bones and liquid
½ raw egg
1 tablespoon [15 mL] tomato, fresh or canned, diced
1 teaspoon [5 mL] parsley, fresh ground (optional)
¼ cup [60 mL] broth if desired

Combine turkey, salmon, and egg in a medium bowl, and mix well. Add tomatoes and parsley, and mix. Add 1 tablespoon of bone broth, if desired. Mix well and shape into a loaf. Place in baking dish. Pour remaining broth, if desired, on top of turkey loaf. Bake in 350-degree oven for 30 minutes or until inside temperature reaches 185°F. Allow to cool and serve.

Hint: Chop cooled hash into bite-size pieces. Add extra broth for added flavor. No need to add calcium to this recipe since the bones in the salmon provide it.

♪ TURKEY & SHRIMP

Protein: 28 grams **Fat:** 11 grams **Calories:** 238
Daily serving for a 10 lb cat; can be divided into 2 feedings.

· ·

½ cup [125 mL] turkey breast cooked, ground or shredded
2 tablespoons [30 mL] chicken liver, cooked, ground fine
3 medium to large shrimp, cooked, tail removed, chopped fine
1 tablespoon [15mL] red beans, cooked, mashed
1 teaspoon [5 mL] cod liver oil
150 mg calcium from a supplement or slightly less than ⅛ tsp
   finely ground eggshell

Combine turkey and liver in medium bowl, and mix well. Add shrimp, mashed beans, cod liver oil, and calcium, and mix. Serve.

Hint: Salad-size shrimp are a less expensive option. If you use salad-size shrimp, use 4 or 5 per large to medium shrimp as a replacement.

DUCK FOR CATS

Duck Casserole

♩ DUCK CASSEROLE

Protein: 15 grams **Fat:** 12 grams **Calories:** 185
Daily serving for a 10 lb cat, can be divided into 2 feedings

. . . .

½ cup [125 mL] duck, cooked, fat and skin removed, ground/
   chopped
1 oyster, canned, mashed
1 teaspoon [5 mL] sunflower seeds, dried, no salt added, ground
   fine
1 teaspoon [5 mL] peas, cooked, mashed
150 mg calcium from a supplement or slightly less than ⅛ tsp
   finely ground eggshell
¼ cup [60 mL] broth, if desired

Combine duck and mashed oyster in medium bowl, and mix well.
Add sunflower seeds, peas, calcium and broth if desired. Mix and
serve.

Hint: Don't be afraid of serving duck to your cat—it's a great
alternative meat protein.

BEEF FOR CATS

Steak & Oysters

Steak & Eggs

Beef & Pumpkin

Beef & Tuna

♪ STEAK & OYSTERS

Protein: 18 grams **Fat:** 8 grams **Calories:** 189
Daily serving for a 10 lb cat, can be divided into 2 feedings.

• •

½ cup [125 mL] beef round roast, or similar, cooked, shredded
   or ground
1 oyster, canned, mashed
1 teaspoon [5 mL] spinach, fresh or frozen, cooked, no salt
   added, chopped fine
2 teaspoons [10 mL] cod liver oil
100 mg calcium from a supplement or slightly less than ¹⁄₁₆
   teaspoon finely ground eggshell
¼ cup [60 mL] broth, if desired

Combine beef and mashed oyster in medium bowl, and mix well.
Add spinach, oil, and calcium, and mix. Add broth, if desired and
mix again. Serve.

Hint: Spinach can color the food light green. Grind the
spinach in a blender for a very fine chop.

♪ STEAK & EGGS

Protein: 23 grams **Fat:** 6 grams **Calories:** 164
Daily serving for a 10 lb cat, can be divided into 2 feedings.

. . . .

½ cup [125 mL] beef round roast, or similar, cooked, shredded
    or ground
1 tablespoon [15 mL] chicken liver, cooked, ground fine
½ egg boiled, chopped
1 teaspoon [5 mL] pumpkin, canned
1 teaspoon [5 mL] sunflower seeds, dried, no salt added, ground
    fine
150 mg calcium from a supplement or slightly less than ⅛
    teaspoon finely ground eggshell
¼ cup [60 mL] broth, if desired

Combine beef, liver, and egg in medium bowl, and mix well. Add
pumpkin, sunflower seeds and calcium, and mix. Add broth if
desired and mix again. Serve.

Hint: Don't throw out the other half of the egg. Either double
the recipe or freeze it for later.

❥ BEEF & PUMPKIN

Protein: 18 grams **Fat:** 9 grams **Calories:** 208
Daily serving for a 10 lb cat, can be divided into 2 feedings.

• •

½ cup [125 mL] beef round roast, or similar, cooked, shredded
or ground
1 teaspoon [5 mL] pumpkin, canned
1 teaspoon [5 mL] sunflower seeds, dried, no salt added, finely
ground
2 teaspoons [10 mL] cod liver oil
100 mg calcium from a supplement or slightly less than ⅟₁₆
teaspoon finely ground eggshell
¼ cup [60 mL] broth, if desired

Combine beef and pumpkin in medium bowl, and mix well. Add
sunflower seeds, oil and calcium, and mix. Add broth if desired and
mix again. Serve.

Hint: Freeze remaining pumpkin in 1- to 2-teaspoon servings.

♪ BEEF & TUNA

Protein: 31 grams **Fat:** 5 grams **Calories:** 185
Daily serving for a 10 lb cat, can be divided into 2 feedings.

· ·

½ cup [125 mL] beef round roast or similar, cooked, shredded
    or ground
1 ½ ounces [45 g] yellow fin tuna, cooked, chopped
1 teaspoon [5 mL] pumpkin, canned
1 teaspoon [5 mL] sunflower seeds, dried, no salt added, ground
1 teaspoon [5 mL] cod liver oil
150 mg calcium from a supplement or slightly less than ⅛ tsp
    finely ground eggshell
¼ cup [60 mL] broth, if desired

Combine beef and tuna in medium bowl, and mix well. Add
pumpkin, sunflower seeds, cod liver oil and calcium, and mix. Add
broth, if desired and mix again. Serve.

Hint: 1 ½ ounces [45 g] of fresh or canned tuna is about ¼ cup
[60 mL].

EGGS FOR CATS

Eggs & Chicken

♪ EGGS & CHICKEN

Protein: 24 grams **Fat:** 23 grams **Calories:** 315
Daily serving for a 10 lb cat, can be divided into 2 feedings.

· ·

2 teaspoons [10 mL] olive oil or butter
2 raw eggs
1 teaspoon [5 mL] milk
¼ cup [60 mL] chicken, cooked, ground
1 tablespoon [15 mL] applesauce, unsweetened
1 teaspoon [5 mL] sunflower seeds, dried, no salt added, finely
    ground
100 mg calcium from a supplement or slightly less than ¹⁄₁₆
    teaspoon finely ground eggshell
¼ cup [60 mL] broth, if desired

Heat skillet over medium heat. Add oil or butter to coat. Combine eggs and milk in medium bowl, mix well. Combine eggs with chicken, applesauce, sunflower seeds and calcium. Add to skillet when oil starts to sizzle. Use silicone spatula to mix and turn. It is finished when egg is no longer runny. Don't overcook—eggs will be dry. Allow to cool. Add broth if desired and serve.

Hint: For variety, substitute salmon or tuna for chicken.

FISH FOR CATS

Fish Salad

Gumbo

Clam Chowder

♪ FISH SALAD

Protein: 19 grams **Fat:** 10 grams **Calories:** 175
Daily serving for a 10 lb cat, can be divided into 2 feedings.

. . . .

¼ cup [60 mL] salmon, pink, canned with bone and liquid, mashed
4 medium to large shrimp, cooked, tail removed
2 tablespoons [30 mL] chicken hearts cooked, chopped fine
1 teaspoon [5 mL] mushrooms lightly steamed, chopped fine
1 teaspoon [5 mL] spinach, fresh or frozen, steamed, chopped fine
1 teaspoon [5 mL] sunflower seeds, dried, no salt added, finely ground
1 teaspoon [5 mL] cod liver oil
¼ cup [60 mL] broth, if desired

Combine salmon, shrimp and chicken hearts in medium bowl, mix well. Add mushrooms, spinach, sunflower seeds and cod liver oil, mix. Add broth if desired and mix again. Serve.

Hint: No need for added calcium in this recipe.

♩ GUMBO

Protein: 34 grams **Fat:** 9 grams **Calories:** 265
Daily serving for a 10 lb cat, can be divided into 2 feedings.

. . . .

½ cup [125 mL] chicken breast, cooked, skin and fat removed,
    ground or shredded
1 tablespoon [15 mL] chicken liver, cooked, finely ground
1 medium to large shrimp, cooked, tail removed, finely chopped
¼ can [50 mL] clams (6.5 oz can) with liquid, chopped
1 teaspoon [5mL] tomatoes, fresh or canned, cooked, finely
    diced
1 tablespoon [15 mL] brown rice, cooked
1 teaspoon [5 mL] cod liver oil
150 mg calcium from a supplement or slightly less than ⅛
    teaspoon finely ground eggshell
¼ cup [60 mL] broth, if desired

Combine chicken, liver, shrimp and clams in medium bowl, mix
well. Add tomatoes, rice, cod liver oil and calcium, mix. Add broth
if desired and mix again. Serve.

Hint: One of the most difficult challenges when preparing cat
food at home is keeping cats out of the bowl during preparation!

⌒CLAM CHOWDER

Protein: 16 grams **Fat:** 10 grams **Calories:** 175
Daily serving for a 10 lb cat, can be divided into 2 feedings.

· ·

½ can [100 mL] (6.5 oz can) clams with liquid, chopped
¼ cup [60 mL] mackerel (or kingfish) cooked, with skin and
   bone, chopped
¼ can [40 mL] (3.75 oz can) sardines, in oil, mashed or chopped
1 tablespoon [15 mL] mushrooms, white, steamed, finely
   chopped
1 tablespoon [15 mL] shredded cheddar cheese
150 mg calcium from a supplement or slightly less than ⅛ tsp
   finely ground eggshell
¼ cup [60 mL] broth, if desired

Combine clams, mackerel and sardines in medium bowl, mix well.
Add mushrooms, cheese and calcium, mix. Add broth if desired,
and mix again. Serve.

> **Hint:** Some cats like chunks of fish, others prefer the food to
> be finely ground. Your cat will let you know its preference.

CHICKEN FOR CATS

Chicken & Rice Casserole

Chicken & Clams

Chicken & Shrimp

Hearty Chicken Stew

Chicken Scallopini

Chicken & Sardines

Chicken & Liver

Chicken & Seafood

Chicken & Pumpkin

♪ CHICKEN & RICE CASSEROLE

Protein: 26 grams **Fat:** 10 grams **Calories:** 235
Daily serving for a 10 lb cat, can be divided into 2 feedings.

• •

½ cup [125 mL] chicken breast, cooked, skin and fat removed, ground or shredded
2 tablespoons [30 mL] chicken liver, cooked, finely ground
1 tablespoon [15 mL] brown rice, cooked
1 teaspoon [5 mL] water chestnuts, canned, finely chopped
1 tablespoon [15 mL] shredded cheddar cheese
1 teaspoon [5 mL] sunflower seeds, dried, no salt added, finely ground
1 teaspoon [5 mL] cod liver oil
150 mg calcium from a supplement or slightly less than ⅛ teaspoon finely ground eggshell
¼ cup [60 mL] broth, if desired

Combine chicken and liver in medium bowl, and mix well. Add rice, water chestnuts and cheese, and mix well. Add sunflower seeds, cod liver oil and calcium, and mix. Add broth if desired and mix again. Serve.

Hint: Water chestnuts for cats? My cats love them—but only if they are chopped into small bits.

♪CHICKEN & CLAMS

Protein: 21 grams **Fat:** 13 grams **Calories:** 312
Daily serving for a 10 lb cat, can be divided into 2 feedings.

. . . .

½ cup [125 mL] chicken breast, cooked, skin and fat removed,
  ground or shredded
½ can [100 mL] (6.5 oz can) clams with liquid, chopped
2 tablespoons [30 mL] chicken liver, cooked, finely ground
1 teaspoon [5 mL] sunflower seeds, dried, no salt added, finely
  ground
2 teaspoons [10 mL] cod liver oil
150 mg calcium from a supplement or slightly less than ⅛
  teaspoon finely ground eggshell
¼ cup [60 mL] broth, if desired

Combine chicken, clams (and liquid) and liver in medium bowl,
mix well. Add sunflower seeds, cod liver oil and calcium and broth
if desired, mix. Serve.

Hint: This is the favorite recipe with my cats!

♪CHICKEN & SHRIMP

Protein: 21 grams **Fat:** 12 grams **Calories:** 200
Daily serving for a 10 lb cat, can be divided into 2 feedings.

. . . .

½ cup [125 mL] chicken breast, cooked, skin and fat removed,
  ground or shredded
3 medium to large shrimp, cooked, tail removed, chopped
1 teaspoon [5 mL] sunflower seeds, dried, no salt added, finely
  ground
1 teaspoon [5 mL] cod liver oil
150 mg calcium from a supplement or slightly less than ⅛
  teaspoon finely ground eggshell
¼ cup [60 mL] broth, if desired

Combine chicken and shrimp in medium bowl, mix well. Add
sunflower seeds, cod liver oil and calcium, mix. Add broth if desired,
mix. Serve.

Hint: Don't hesitate to use extra broth (home-prepared only).
Cats love it and benefit from the added moisture in their diet.

♪HEARTY CHICKEN STEW

Protein: 18 grams **Fat:** 12 grams **Calories:** 193
Daily serving for a 10 lb cat, can be divided into 2 feedings.

. . . .

½ cup [125 mL] chicken breast, cooked, skin and fat removed, ground or shredded
½ can [100 mL] (6.5 oz can) clams with liquid, chopped
1 tablespoon [15 mL] parsley, fresh, finely chopped
1 teaspoon [5 mL] sunflower seeds, dried, no salt added, finely ground
2 teaspoons [10 mL] cod liver oil
150 mg calcium from a supplement or slightly less than ⅛ teaspoon finely ground eggshell
¼ cup [60 mL] broth, if desired

Combine chicken and clams in medium bowl, mix well. Add parsley, sunflower seeds, cod liver oil and calcium, mix. Add broth if desired, mix. Serve.

Hint: Fresh parsley adds flavor and nutrition!

♪ CHICKEN SCALLOPINI

Protein: 25 grams **Fat:** 10 grams **Calories:** 210
Daily serving for a 10 lb cat, can be divided into 2 feedings.

. . . .

½ cup [125 mL] chicken breast, cooked, skin and fat removed, ground or shredded
2 tablespoons [30 mL] chicken liver, cooked, finely ground
1 teaspoon [5 mL] mushrooms, steamed, finely chopped
1 tablespoon [15 mL] whole wheat pasta, cooked, finely chopped
1 teaspoon [5 mL] sunflower seeds, dried, no salt added, finely ground
1 teaspoon [5 mL] cod liver oil
150 mg calcium from a supplement or slightly less than ⅛ teaspoon finely ground eggshell
¼ cup [60 mL] broth, if desired

Combine chicken and liver in medium bowl, mix well. Add mushrooms, pasta, sunflower seeds, cod liver oil and calcium, mix. Add broth if desired, mix. Serve.

Hint: Use any variety of whole wheat pasta.

♪ CHICKEN & SARDINES

Protein: 34 grams **Fat:** 10 grams **Calories:** 245
Daily serving for a 10 lb cat, can be divided into 2 feedings.

. . . .

½ cup [125 mL] chicken breast, cooked, skin and fat removed, ground or shredded
1 tablespoon [15 mL] chicken liver, cooked, ground
½ can [50 mL] (3.75 oz can) sardines in oil, mashed
1 teaspoon [5 mL] sunflower seeds, dried, no salt added, finely ground
¼ cup [60 mL] broth, if desired

Combine chicken, liver and sardines in medium bowl, mix well. Add sunflower seeds, mix. Add broth if desired, mix. Serve.

Hint: No need to add calcium to this recipe; the bones in the sardines provide it. Select sardines in olive oil or tomato sauce.

🐾CHICKEN & LIVER

Protein: 25 grams **Fat:** 14 grams **Calories:** 231
Daily serving for a 10 lb cat, can be divided into 2 feedings.

· ·

½ cup [125 mL] chicken breast, cooked, skin and fat removed, ground or shredded

2 tablespoons [30 mL] chicken liver, cooked, ground

1 teaspoon [5 mL] sunflower seeds, dried, no salt added, finely ground

1 teaspoon [5 mL] cod liver oil

150 mg calcium from a supplement or slightly less than ⅛ teaspoon finely ground eggshell

¼ cup [60 mL] broth, if desired

Combine chicken and liver in medium bowl, mix well. Add sunflower seeds, cod liver oil and calcium, mix. Add broth if desired, mix. Serve.

Hint: Very popular recipe and easy to make.

♪CHICKEN & SEAFOOD

Protein: 33 grams **Fat:** 8 grams **Calories:** 230
Daily serving for a 10 lb cat, can be divided into 2 feedings.

· ·

½ cup [125 mL] chicken breast, cooked, skin and fat removed, ground or shredded
1 tablespoon [15 mL] chicken heart, cooked, ground
¼ cup [60 mL] salmon, pink, canned with bone and liquid, mashed
¼ can [50 mL] (3.75 oz can) sardines in oil, mashed
1 tablespoon [15 mL] broccoli, fresh or frozen, cooked, finely chopped
1 tablespoon [15 mL] pumpkin, canned
¼ cup [60 mL] broth, if desired

Combine chicken, heart, salmon and sardines in medium bowl, mix well. Add broccoli and pumpkin, mix. Add broth if desired, mix. Serve.

Hint: Calcium does not need to be added to this recipe.

♪CHICKEN & PUMPKIN

Protein: 21 grams **Fat:** 15 grams **Calories:** 238
Daily serving for a 10 lb cat, can be divided into 2 feedings.

• •

½ cup [125 mL] chicken breast, cooked, skin and fat removed, ground or shredded
1 tablespoon [15 mL] chicken heart, cooked, ground
1 teaspoon [5 mL] pumpkin, canned
1 teaspoon [5 mL] sunflower seeds, dried, no salt added, finely ground
2 teaspoons [10 mL] cod liver oil
150 mg calcium from a supplement or slightly less than ⅛ teaspoon finely ground eggshell
¼ cup [60 mL] broth, if desired

Combine chicken and heart in medium bowl, mix well. Add pumpkin, sunflower seeds, oil and calcium, mix. Add broth if desired, mix. Serve.

Hint: Organic canned pumpkin is available in many grocery stores.

DOGS

TURKEY FOR DOGS

Turkey, Shrimp & Black Beans

Turkey Dinner

Turkey & Oats

Turkey & Salmon Hash

Turkey Meatloaf

TURKEY, SHRIMP & BLACK BEANS

Protein: 54 grams **Fat:** 13 grams **Calories:** 589
Daily serving for a 30 lb dog, can be divided into 2 feedings.

. . . .

½ cup [125 mL] turkey breast, cooked, skin and fat removed, ground or shredded
2 tablespoons [30 mL] chicken liver, cooked, finely ground
4 medium to large shrimp, cooked, tail removed, chopped
1 ½ cups [375 mL] black beans, cooked, mashed
¾ cup [175 mL] cauliflower, fresh or frozen, steamed, chopped
¼ cup [60 mL] alfalfa sprouts
1 teaspoon [5 mL] cod liver oil
500 mg calcium from a supplement or slightly more than ¼ teaspoon finely ground eggshell
½ cup [125 mL] broth, if desired

Combine turkey, liver, shrimp and calcium in medium bowl, mix well. Add cauliflower, sprouts and cod liver oil, mix. Add broth if desired, mix. Add beans last, mix gently and serve.

> **Hint**: Black beans cook slowly. Make sure they are soft and will mash easily with a fork before serving. They freeze well; as a time saver prepare a large batch of beans and freeze individual portions.

🐕 TURKEY DINNER

Protein: 40 grams **Fat:** 15 grams **Calories:** 577
Daily serving for a 30 lb dog, can be divided into 2 feedings.

. . . .

½ cup [125 mL] turkey breast, cooked, skin and fat removed,
   ground or shredded
2 tablespoons [30 mL] chicken liver, cooked, finely ground
¾ cup [175 mL] sweet potato, cooked with skin, chopped
¾ cup [175 mL] cauliflower, fresh or frozen, steamed, chopped
¾ cup [175 mL] broccoli, steamed, chopped
½ cup [125 mL] mushrooms, steamed, chopped
1 cup [250 mL] black beans, cooked, mashed
2 teaspoons [10 mL] sunflower seeds, dried, no salt added,
   whole or finely ground
2 teaspoons [10 mL] olive oil
500 mg calcium from a supplement or slightly more than ¼
   teaspoon finely ground eggshell
½ cup [125 mL] broth, if desired

Combine turkey, chicken liver, sweet potato, cauliflower, broccoli
and mushroom in medium bowl, mix well. Add sunflower seeds,
oil and calcium, mix. Add broth if desired, mix. Add beans last, mix
gently and serve.

Hint: Adding beans last and mixing gently prevents the dog
food from appearing gray from mashed beans. And don't be
too surprised to see your pets' stools become colored from the
ingredients; it's natural.

🐕 TURKEY & OATS

Protein: 50 grams **Fat:** 21 grams **Calories:** 853
Daily serving for a 30 lb dog, can be divided into 2 feedings.

. . . .

1 cup [250 mL] steel cut oats
4 cups [1000 mL] water
½ cup [125 mL] berries (blueberries, strawberries, hawthorne)
½ cup [125 mL] broccoli, chopped
Dash of cinnamon
½ cup [125 mL] turkey, raw, ground, frozen
500 mg calcium from a supplement or slightly more than ¼
    teaspoon finely ground eggshell
½ cup [125 mL] broth, if desired

Place the oats, water, berries, broccoli and cinnamon in a slow
cooker on low overnight. In the morning, turn off the slow cooker,
place the frozen chunk of meat in the mixture and wait 30 minutes.
Stir. Everything will come to a good temperature to serve, the meat
will be slightly cooked and the mixture will be cooled down. Before
serving, add calcium and then broth, if desired.

Hint: You can use fresh ground turkey instead of frozen.

TURKEY & SALMON HASH

Protein: 39 grams **Fat:** 24 grams **Calories:** 488
Daily serving for a 30 lb dog, can be divided into 2 feedings.

- -

½ cup [125 mL] turkey, raw, ground
¼ cup [60 mL] salmon, pink, canned
½ raw egg
½ cup [125 mL] tomatoes, canned or fresh, diced
¼ cup [60 mL] sweet potato, raw, chopped
¼ cup [60 mL] broccoli, raw, chopped
½ cup [125 mL] red beans, cooked
2 teaspoons [10 mL] sunflower seeds, dried, no salt added, whole or finely ground
1 teaspoon [5 mL] olive oil
400 mg calcium from a supplement or slightly more than ¼ teaspoon finely ground eggshell
½ cup [125 mL] broth, if desired

Combine turkey, salmon and egg in a medium bowl, mix well. Add tomatoes, sweet potato, broccoli, sunflower seeds, oil and calcium, mix. Add ¼ cup of broth, if using. Add beans and mix well. Shape into a loaf. Place in baking dish. Add remaining broth, if using, on top. Bake in 350-degree oven for 30 minutes or until inside temperature of loaf reaches 185 degrees. Allow to cool and serve.

Hint: Once the hash is cooked and cooled, chop into bite-size pieces to serve.

⋔TURKEY MEATLOAF

Protein: 52 grams **Fat:** 30 grams **Calories:** 550
Daily serving for a 30 lb dog, can be divided into 2 feedings.

· ·

½ cup [125 mL] turkey, raw, ground
½ cup [125 mL] salmon, pink, canned with bone and liquid
1 raw egg
¾ cup [175 mL] cauliflower, fresh or frozen, chopped
¾ cup [175 mL] broccoli, fresh or frozen, chopped
¾ cup [175 mL] peas, fresh or frozen
2 teaspoons [10 mL] sunflower seeds, dried, no salt added, whole or finely ground
1 teaspoon [5 mL] cod liver oil
400 mg calcium from a supplement or slightly more than ¼ teaspoon finely ground eggshell
½ cup [125 mL] broth, if desired

Combine turkey, salmon and egg in a medium bowl, mix well. Add cauliflower, broccoli, peas, sunflower seeds, oil and calcium, mix. Add ¼ cup of broth, if using and mix. Shape into a loaf. Place in baking dish. Add remaining broth, if using, on top. Bake in 350-degree oven for 30 minutes or until inside temperature of loaf reaches 185 degrees. Allow to cool and serve.

Hint: Always use a meat thermometer. This prevents under- or over-cooking.

DUCK FOR DOGS

Duck Casserole

⚞DUCK CASSEROLE

Protein: 36 grams **Fat:** 18 grams **Calories:** 525
Daily serving for a 30 lb dog, can be divided into 2 feedings.

· ·

½ cup [125 mL] duck, cooked, skin and fat removed, ground
   or shredded
2 tablespoons [30 mL] chicken liver, cooked, ground
3 oysters, canned, mashed
1 egg, hard-boiled
1 cup [250 mL] mushrooms, white, steamed, chopped
½ cup [125 mL] sweet potato, with skin, diced
½ cup [125 mL] peas, steamed
½ cup [125 mL] brown rice, cooked
2 teaspoons [10 mL] cod liver oil
400 mg calcium from a supplement or slightly more than ¼
   teaspoon finely ground eggshell
½ cup [125 mL] broth, if desired

Combine duck, liver, oysters and egg in medium bowl, mix well.
Add mushrooms, sweet potatoes, peas, rice, oil and calcium, mix.
Add broth, if using, mix again and serve.

Hint: Duck provides a great alternative meat protein, especially
for those with allergies.

BEEF FOR DOGS

Beef Stroganoff

Spaghetti

Beef Stew

Meatloaf

Lasagna

Beef & Veggies

Beef, Egg & Rice

Chili

Mutt Burger

🐕 BEEF STROGANOFF

Protein: 38 grams **Fat:** 19 grams **Calories:** 510
Daily serving for a 30 lb dog, can be divided into 2 feedings.

• •

½ cup [125 mL] beef, cooked and shredded
2 tablespoons [30 mL] chicken liver, cooked, ground
3 oysters, canned, mashed
½ cup [125 mL] cauliflower, steamed, chopped
½ cup [125 mL] green beans, steamed
½ cup [125 mL] white mushrooms, lightly steamed
1 cup [250 mL] whole wheat pasta, cooked
1 teaspoon [5 mL] cod liver oil
600 mg calcium from a supplement or slightly more than ¼
    teaspoon finely ground eggshell
½ cup [125 mL] broth, if desired

Combine beef, liver and oysters in medium bowl, mix well. Add cauliflower, green beans, mushrooms, oil and calcium, mix. Add broth, if using, mix. Add pasta last, mix gently and serve.

Hint: Some varieties of whole wheat pasta tend to stick. To prevent sticking, add 1 teaspoon of olive oil to water before boiling.

🐕 SPAGHETTI

Protein: 44 grams **Fat:** 22 grams **Calories:** 600
Daily serving for a 30 lb dog, can be divided into 2 feedings.

. . . .

½ cup [125 mL] beef, cooked and shredded
4 tablespoons [60 mL] beef liver, cooked, ground
1 cup [250 mL] tomatoes, fresh or canned, cooked, diced
½ cup [125 mL] cauliflower, steamed, chopped
½ cup [125 mL] mushrooms, steamed, chopped
1 cup [250 mL] whole wheat spaghetti noodles, cooked
600 mg calcium from a supplement or slightly more than ¼
    teaspoon finely ground eggshell
½ cup [125 mL] broth, if desired

Combine beef and liver in medium bowl, mix well. Add tomatoes, cauliflower and mushrooms, mix. Add calcium and broth, if using, mix. Add pasta last, mix gently and serve.

Hint: Don't hesitate to add more vegetables to any recipe. For dogs with large appetites, additional vegetables provide extra bulk but not a lot of extra calories.

🐕BEEF STEW

Protein: 34 grams **Fat:** 15 grams **Calories:** 480
Daily serving for a 30 lb dog, can be divided into 2 feedings.

• •

½ cup [125 mL] beef, cooked, cubed
1 cup [250 mL] black beans, cooked
1 cup [250 mL] mixed vegetables
2 teaspoons [10 mL] cod liver oil
500 mg calcium from a supplement or slightly more than ¼
teaspoon finely ground eggshell

Cover and soak beans overnight in water. Cook beans in slow cooker until tender, about 12–24 hours. Add beef, mixed vegetables and cod liver oil. Cook for 1–2 more hours until vegetables are tender. Add calcium. Serve.

Hint: Use frozen or fresh vegetables. This is a great recipe to double or triple in the slow cooker.

🐕 MEATLOAF

Protein: 32 grams **Fat:** 20 grams **Calories:** 550
Daily serving for a 30 lb dog, can be divided into 2 feedings.

. . . .

½ cup [125 mL] lean ground beef, raw
1 cup [250 mL] brown rice, cooked
2 cups [500 mL] mixed vegetables, fresh or frozen
1 raw egg
1 teaspoon [5 mL] cod liver oil
500 mg calcium from a supplement or slightly more than ¼
     teaspoon finely ground eggshell
½ cup [125 mL] broth, if desired

Combine all ingredients in a large bowl and mix well. Place into loaf pan and bake at 350 degrees for an hour. Allow to cool and serve.

Hint: When using frozen mixed vegetables, be sure they do NOT include onions. No onions for dogs or cats!

🐕LASAGNA

Protein: 47 grams **Fat:** 30 grams **Calories:** 600
Daily serving for a 30 lb dog, can be divided into 2 feedings.

. . . .

½ cup [125 mL] beef, cooked, ground or shredded
2 tablespoons [30 mL] beef liver, cooked, ground
½ cup [125 mL] tomatoes, fresh or canned, cooked, diced
½ cup [125 mL] green beans, steamed
Olive oil for pan
½ cup [125 mL] whole wheat lasagna noodles, cooked
½ cup [125 mL] mozzarella cheese, low fat, shredded
¼ cup [60 mL] broth

Combine beef, liver, tomatoes and green beans in medium bowl, mix well. Rub olive oil on bottom of a 9x9 baking dish. Layer ingredients in this order from bottom up: noodle, beef and vegetable mixture, cheese. Repeat for two more layers. Pour broth over entire dish. Bake at 350 degrees for 25 to 30 minutes. Allow to cool, serve.

Hint: No need to add calcium to this recipe, the cheese provides it.

🐕 BEEF & VEGGIES

Protein: 33 grams **Fat:** 27 grams **Calories:** 570
Daily serving for a 30 lb dog, can be divided into 2 feedings.

· ·

½ cup [125 mL] beef, cooked and shredded
2 tablespoons [30 mL] beef liver, cooked, ground
½ cup [125 mL] carrots, steamed, chopped
½ cup [125 mL] sweet potato, cooked with skin, diced
½ cup [125 mL] spinach, fresh or frozen, boiled, chopped
½ cup [125 mL] peas, steamed
½ cup [125 mL] brown rice, cooked
2 teaspoons [10 mL] olive oil
400 mg calcium from a supplement or slightly more than ¼
     teaspoon finely ground eggshell
½ cup [125 mL] broth, if desired

Combine beef and liver in medium bowl, mix well. Add carrots, sweet potato, spinach, peas, rice, oil and calcium, mix. Add broth, if using, mix and serve.

Hint: Cut vegetables into size-appropriate bites for your dog.

⚑BEEF, EGG & RICE

Protein: 35 grams **Fat:** 27 grams **Calories:** 600
Daily serving for a 30 lb dog, can be divided into 2 feedings.

. . . .

½ cup [125 mL] beef, cooked and shredded
2 tablespoons [30 mL] beef liver, cooked, ground
1 egg, hard-boiled
½ cup [125 mL] broccoli, steamed, chopped
½ cup [125 mL] cauliflower, steamed, chopped
1 cup [250 mL] brown rice, cooked
1 teaspoon [5 mL] olive oil
400 mg calcium from a supplement or slightly more than ¼
    teaspoon finely ground eggshell
½ cup [125 mL] broth, if desired

Combine beef and liver in medium bowl, mix well. Add rice, egg,
broccoli, cauliflower, oil and calcium, mix. Add broth, if using,
mix and serve.

Hint: Don't overcook vegetables; light steaming provides
optimal nutrition.

⚓CHILI

Protein: 27 grams **Fat:** 13 grams **Calories:** 510
Daily serving for a 30 lb dog, can be divided into 2 feedings.

• •

¼ pound [60 mL] lean ground beef
Olive oil for frying
½ cup [125 mL] cabbage, chopped
½ cup [125 mL] sweet potato, with or without skin, diced
½ cup [125 mL] brown rice
½ cup [125 mL] tomato, diced
½ cup [125 mL] tomato juice
½ cup [125 mL] apple juice
500 mg calcium from a supplement or slightly more than ¼
    teaspoon finely ground eggshell
½ cup [125 mL] broth, if desired

Sauté beef and cabbage in olive oil. Drain fat. Add remaining ingredients and bring to a boil. Turn down to simmer for 1 hour, add water as needed. Allow to cool and serve.

Hint: Serve in a bowl, it's chili!

MUTT BURGER

Protein: 35 grams **Fat:** 22 grams **Calories:** 490
Daily serving for a 30 lb dog, can be divided into 2 feedings.

• •

¼ pound [60 mL] lean ground beef, raw
½ raw egg
¼ cup [60 mL] raw oats
½ cup [125 mL] broccoli, raw, chopped fine
½ cup [125 mL] cauliflower, raw, chopped fine
½ cup [125 mL] carrots, raw, chopped fine
⅛ cup [30 mL] shredded cheddar cheese
500 mg calcium from a supplement or slightly more than ¼
    teaspoon finely ground eggshell

Combine all ingredients in a large bowl, mix well and form into patties. Grill until center is no longer pink. Allow to cool and serve.

Hint: This is a great recipe to double or triple. It freezes well. Burger size is up to you.

EGGS FOR DOGS

Scrambled Eggs, Bacon & Sweet Potato Hash Browns

Scrambled Eggs & Fruit

SCRAMBLED EGGS, BACON & SWEET POTATO HASH BROWNS

Protein: 19 grams **Fat:** 26 grams **Calories:** 410
Daily serving for a 30 lb dog, can be divided into 2 feedings.

. . . .

1 tablespoon [15 mL] olive oil or butter
3 raw eggs
Splash [5 mL] milk
½ cup [125 mL] mushrooms, chopped
½ cup [125 mL] tomato, fresh or canned, diced
2 slices bacon, cooked
1 cup [250 mL] sweet potato, peeled, cooked and diced
400 mg calcium from a supplement or slightly more than ¼
    teaspoon finely ground eggshell

Heat skillet over medium heat. Add oil or butter to coat pan. Combine eggs and milk in medium bowl, mix well, add mushrooms and tomato. Add to skillet when oil starts to sizzle. Use silicone spatula to mix and turn. It is finished when egg mixture is no longer runny. Don't overcook or eggs will be dry and lose some nutrition. Fry bacon as you would for yourself.

Hash browns: placed peeled, diced sweet potato in water, bring to a boil and cook for 3 minutes. Turn off heat. Drain and allow to cool.

Combine cooked sweet potato with eggs and bacon, sprinkle on the calcium, mix, and serve.

Hint: This is a great breakfast for your dog. For variety, substitute ¼ cup [60 mL] canned salmon for bacon.

⚞SCRAMBLED EGGS & FRUIT

Protein: 13 grams **Fat:** 19 grams **Calories:** 480
Daily serving for a 30 lb dog, can be divided into 2 feedings.

· ·

1 tablespoon [15 mL] olive oil or butter
3 raw eggs
Splash [5 mL] milk
¼ cup cooked [60 mL] oats
½ banana
¼ cup [60 mL] blueberries, fresh or frozen
1 tablespoon [15 mL] almond butter
500 mg calcium from a supplement or slightly more than ¼
    teaspoon finely ground eggshell
½ cup [125 mL] broth, if desired

Heat skillet over medium heat. Add oil or butter to coat pan.
Combine eggs and milk in medium bowl, mix well. Add to skillet
when oil starts to sizzle. Use silicone spatula to mix and turn. It is
finished when egg mixture is no longer runny. Don't overcook or
eggs will be dry and lose some nutrition. Combine cooked oats,
banana, blueberries, almond butter, calcium and broth and serve
over eggs.

> **Hint:** This is a healthy breakfast or dinner for your dog—fresh
> fruit is a great source of antioxidants.

FISH FOR DOGS

Fish Salad

Gumbo

Clam Chowder

𝕸FISH SALAD

Protein: 41 grams **Fat:** 13 grams **Calories:** 480
Daily serving for a 30 lb dog, can be divided into 2 feedings.

· ·

½ cup [125 mL] salmon, pink, canned with bone and liquid
4 medium to large shrimp, cooked, tail removed, chopped
2 tablespoons [30 mL] chicken liver, cooked, ground
½ cup [125 mL] white mushrooms, cooked, chopped
½ cup [125 mL] spinach, fresh or frozen, chopped
½ cup [125 mL] green beans, fresh or frozen, steamed
½ cup [125 mL] carrots, steamed, chopped
1 teaspoon [5 mL] cod liver oil
300 mg calcium from a supplement or slightly more than ⅛
     teaspoon finely ground eggshell
½ cup [125 mL] broth, if desired
1 cup [250 mL] whole wheat pasta, cooked

Combine salmon, shrimp and liver in medium bowl, mix well. Add mushrooms, spinach, green beans, carrots, oil and calcium, mix. Add broth if using and pasta. Gently mix again and serve.

Hint: Salad-size shrimp, which are less expensive, can be substituted for medium to large shrimp.

♞GUMBO

• •

½ cup [125 mL] chicken breast, cooked, skin and fat removed, ground or shredded
4 medium to large shrimp, cooked, tail removed, chopped
2 tablespoons [30 mL] chicken liver, cooked, ground
½ can (6.5 oz can) clams, with liquid, chopped
½ cup [125 mL] tomatoes, fresh or canned, cooked, diced
½ cup [125 mL] celery, steamed, chopped
1 cup [250 mL] brown rice, cooked
2 teaspoons [10 mL] cod liver oil
400 mg calcium from a supplement or slightly more than ¼ teaspoon finely ground eggshell
½ cup [125 mL] broth, if desired

Combine chicken, liver, shrimp and clams in medium bowl, mix well. Add tomatoes, celery, rice, oil and calcium, mix. Add broth if using and mix again. Serve.

Hint: Add extra tomatoes and celery for big appetites.

🐕CLAM CHOWDER

Protein: 28 grams **Fat:** 24 grams **Calories:** 430
Daily serving for a 30 lb dog, can be divided into 2 feedings.

· ·

1 can [100 mL] (6.5 oz can) clams, with liquid, chopped
½ can [40 mL] (3.75 oz can) sardines in oil, mashed
2 tablespoons [30 mL] chicken hearts, cooked, ground
½ cup [125 mL] peas, cooked
½ cup [125 mL] apple, raw, peeled, cored, chopped
½ cup [125 mL] cauliflower, fresh or frozen, steamed, chopped
½ cup [125 mL] sweet potato, in skin, cooked, diced
2 teaspoons [10 mL] sunflower seeds, dried, no salt added,
     whole or finely ground
1 teaspoon [5 mL] cod liver oil
300 mg calcium from a supplement or slightly more than ⅛
     teaspoon finely ground eggshell
½ cup [125 mL] broth, if desired

Combine clams, sardines and chicken hearts in medium bowl, mix well. Add peas, apple, cauliflower, sweet potato, sunflower seeds, oil and calcium, mix. Add broth if using and mix again. Serve.

Hint: Apple can be added raw or lightly steamed.

CHICKEN FOR DOGS

Hearty Chicken Stew

Chicken & Fish

Chicken, Shrimp & Veggies

Chicken & Rice Casserole

Chicken, Vegetables & Rice Casserole

Chicken Noodleroni

Chicken Scallopini

Chicken & Tuna

Chicken & Sardines

⚘HEARTY CHICKEN STEW

Protein: 41 grams **Fat:** 19 grams **Calories:** 560
Daily serving for a 30 lb dog, can be divided into 2 feedings.

. . . .

½ cup [125 mL] chicken, cooked, skin and fat removed, ground
or shredded
2 tablespoons [30 mL] chicken liver, cooked, ground
½ can [50 mL] (6.5 oz can) clams, with liquid, chopped
1 hard-boiled egg, chopped
½ cup [125 mL] celery, steamed, chopped
½ cup [125 mL] tomatoes, steamed, chopped
½ cup [125 mL] mushrooms, steamed, chopped
½ cup [125 mL] cauliflower, steamed, chopped
1 tablespoon [15 mL] parsley, fresh, chopped
2 teaspoons [10 mL] cod liver oil
400 mg calcium from a supplement or slightly more than ⅛
teaspoon finely ground eggshell
½ cup [125 mL] broth, if desired
1 cup [250 mL] whole wheat pasta, cooked

Combine chicken, chicken liver, clams and egg in medium bowl, mix well. Add celery, tomatoes, mushrooms, cauliflower, parsley, oil and calcium, mix. Add pasta and broth, if using, and mix again. Serve.

Hint: Chop parsley fine, all other vegetables can be chopped in bite-appropriate size.

🐕 CHICKEN & FISH

Protein: 41 grams **Fat:** 17 grams **Calories:** 500
Daily serving for a 30 lb dog, can be divided into 2 feedings.

· ·

¼ cup [60 mL] chicken breast, cooked, skin and fat removed, ground or shredded
1 tablespoon [15 mL] chicken hearts, cooked, ground
4 oysters, canned, mashed
¼ cup [60 mL] salmon, pink, canned, with bone and liquid, chopped
¼ cup [60 mL] spinach, fresh or frozen, steamed, chopped
¼ cup [60 mL] mushrooms, white, steamed, chopped
1 teaspoon [5 mL] sunflower seeds, dried, no salt added, whole or finely ground
2 teaspoons [10 mL] cod liver oil
300 mg calcium from a supplement or slightly more than ⅛ teaspoon finely ground eggshell
½ cup [125 mL] broth, if desired
1 cup [250 mL] black beans, cooked

Combine chicken, chicken hearts, oysters and salmon in medium bowl, mix well. Add spinach, mushrooms, sunflower seeds, oil and calcium, mix. Add broth, if using, and beans and mix again. Serve.

> **Hint:** Black beans are slow to cook, make sure they are soft before serving. Some foods, such as black beans, can color dog stool, so don't be shocked at what you find in the back yard.

CHICKEN, SHRIMP & VEGGIES

Protein: 45 grams **Fat:** 15 grams **Calories:** 550
Daily serving for a 30 lb dog, can be divided into 2 feedings.

. . . .

½ cup [125 mL] chicken breast, cooked, skin and fat removed, ground or shredded
2 tablespoons [30 mL] chicken liver, cooked, ground
6 medium to large shrimp, cooked, tail removed, chopped
½ cup [125 mL] cabbage, cooked, shredded
½ cup [125 mL] peas, cooked
½ cup [125 mL] cauliflower, fresh or frozen, cooked, chopped
½ cup [125 mL] apple, raw, peeled, cored, chopped
2 teaspoons [10 mL] cod liver oil
400 mg calcium from a supplement or slightly more than ⅛ teaspoon finely ground eggshell
½ cup [125 mL] broth, if desired
1 cup [250 mL] whole wheat pasta, cooked

Combine chicken, liver and shrimp in medium bowl, mix well. Add cabbage, peas, cauliflower, apple, oil and calcium, mix. Add broth, if using, and pasta and mix again. Serve.

Hint: Lots of great nutrition in this recipe!

CHICKEN & RICE CASSEROLE

Protein: 40 grams **Fat:** 24 grams **Calories:** 660
Daily serving for a 30 lb dog, can be divided into 2 feedings.

. . . .

½ cup [125 mL] chicken breast, cooked, skin and fat removed,
    ground or shredded
2 tablespoons [30 mL] chicken liver, cooked, ground
½ cup [125 mL] green beans, fresh or frozen, steamed, chopped
½ can [50 mL] (8 oz can) water chestnuts, with liquid, chopped
½ cup [125 mL] mushrooms, white, steamed, chopped
¼ cup [60 mL] cheddar cheese, shredded
¾ cup [175 mL] brown rice, cooked
1 teaspoon [5 mL] cod liver oil
400 mg calcium from a supplement or slightly more than ⅛
    teaspoon finely ground eggshell
½ cup [125 mL] broth, if desired

Combine chicken and liver in medium bowl, mix well. Add green
beans, water chestnuts, mushrooms, cheese, rice, oil and calcium,
mix. Add broth, if using, and mix again. Serve.

Hint: Add more vegetables and less cheese for overweight dogs.

🐕CHICKEN, VEGETABLES & RICE CASSEROLE

Protein: 35 grams **Fat:** 15 grams **Calories:** 530
Daily serving for a 30 lb dog, can be divided into 2 feedings.

· ·

½ cup [125 mL] chicken breast, cooked, skin and fat removed, ground or shredded
2 tablespoons [30 mL] chicken liver, cooked, ground
½ cup [125 mL] broccoli, fresh or frozen, steamed, chopped
½ cup [125 mL] cauliflower, fresh or frozen, steamed, chopped
½ cup [125 mL] sweet potato, in skin, cooked, diced
½ cup [125 mL] spinach, fresh or frozen, steamed, chopped
1 cup [250 mL] brown rice, cooked
2 teaspoons [10 mL] cod liver oil
400 mg calcium from a supplement or slightly more than ⅛ teaspoon finely ground eggshell
½ cup [125 mL] broth, if desired

Combine chicken and liver in medium bowl, mix well. Add broccoli, cauliflower, sweet potato, spinach, rice, oil and calcium, mix. Add broth, if using, and mix again. Serve.

Hint: Spinach might color the food a bit, don't worry—it's a natural food coloring.

🐕CHICKEN NOODLERONI

Protein: 36 grams **Fat:** 16 grams **Calories:** 500
Daily serving for a 30 lb dog, can be divided into 2 feedings.

. . . .

½ cup [125 mL] chicken breast, cooked, skin and fat removed,
  ground or shredded
2 tablespoons [30 mL] chicken liver, cooked, ground
¾ cup [175 mL] tomatoes, steamed, chopped
¾ cup [175 mL] peas, steamed
2 teaspoons [10 mL] cod liver oil
400 mg calcium from a supplement or slightly more than ⅛
  teaspoon finely ground eggshell
½ cup [125 mL] broth, if desired
1 cup [250 mL] whole wheat pasta, cooked

Combine chicken and liver in medium bowl, mix well. Add tomatoes, peas, oil and calcium, mix. Add broth, if using, and pasta, and mix again. Serve.

Hint: This recipe looks so yummy, you might not believe that it's dog food!

🐕CHICKEN SCALLOPINI

Protein: 41 grams **Fat:** 16 grams **Calories:** 540
Daily serving for a 30 lb dog, can be divided into 2 feedings.

• •

½ cup [125 mL] chicken breast, cooked, skin and fat removed, ground or shredded
2 tablespoons [30 mL] chicken liver, cooked, ground
¾ cup [175 mL] mushrooms, steamed, chopped
¾ cup [175 mL] red pepper, steamed, chopped
¾ cup [175 mL] peas, steamed
1 cup [250 mL] yogurt, plain, low fat
2 teaspoons [10 mL] cod liver oil
400 mg calcium from a supplement or slightly more than ⅛ teaspoon finely ground eggshell
½ cup [125 mL] broth, if desired
1 cup [250 mL] whole wheat pasta, cooked

Combine chicken and liver in medium bowl, mix well. Add mushrooms, red peppers, peas, yogurt, oil and calcium, mix. Add broth, if using, and pasta and mix again. Serve.

Hint: Use any variety of whole wheat pasta.

⚔CHICKEN & TUNA

Protein: 46 grams **Fat:** 15 grams **Calories:** 500
Daily serving for a 30 lb dog, can be divided into 2 feedings.

· ·

½ cup [125 mL] chicken breast, cooked, skin and fat removed,
  ground or shredded
¼ cup [60 mL] yellow fin tuna, cooked, chopped
2 tablespoons [30 mL] chicken liver, cooked, ground
½ cup [125 mL] green beans, fresh or frozen, steamed, chopped
½ cup [125 mL] cauliflower, fresh or frozen, cooked, chopped
½ cup [125 mL] pumpkin, canned
¾ cup [175 mL] brown rice, cooked
1 teaspoon [5 mL] cod liver oil
400 mg calcium from a supplement or slightly more than ⅛
  teaspoon finely ground eggshell
½ cup [125 mL] broth, if desired

Combine chicken, liver and tuna in medium bowl, mix well. Add
green beans, cauliflower, pumpkin, rice, oil and calcium, mix. Add
broth, if using, and mix again. Serve.

Hint: Leftover pumpkin and fresh vegetables can be frozen in
serving-size portions.

CHICKEN & SARDINES

Protein: 36 grams **Fat:** 15 grams **Calories:** 550
Daily serving for a 30 lb dog, can be divided into 2 feedings.

. . . .

½ cup [125 mL] chicken, cooked, skin and fat removed, ground or shredded
2 tablespoons [30 mL] chicken liver, cooked, ground
½ can [40 mL] (3.75 oz can) sardines, in oil, mashed
1 hard-boiled egg, chopped
½ cup [125 mL] broccoli, fresh or frozen, steamed, chopped
½ cup [125 mL] green beans, fresh or frozen, steamed, chopped
½ cup [125 mL] cauliflower, fresh or frozen, steamed, chopped
1 teaspoon [5 mL] sunflower seeds, dried, no salt added, whole or finely ground
2 teaspoons [10 mL] cod liver oil
300 mg calcium from a supplement or slightly more than ⅛ teaspoon finely ground eggshell
½ cup [125 mL] broth, if desired

Combine chicken, chicken liver, and sardines in medium bowl, mix well. Add cauliflower, broccoli, green beans, sunflower seeds, oil and calcium, mix. Add broth, if using, and mix again. Serve.

Hint: Most dogs love the crunch of whole sunflower seeds.

GRAIN-FREE RECIPES FOR DOGS

Beef, Squash & Beans

Beef & Zucchini

Chicken, Squash, Asparagus & Greens

Healthy PAWSibilities Blend

Salmon & Cabbage

🐕 BEEF, SQUASH & BEANS

Protein: 45 grams **Fat:** 32 grams **Calories:** 330
Daily serving for a 30 lb dog, can be divided into 2 feedings.

• •

⅓ cup [75 mL] lean beef round roast, cooked
1 tablespoon [15 mL] beef liver, cooked, ground
1 hard-boiled egg
2 tablespoons [30 mL] mozzarella or provolone cheese, shredded
½ cup [125 mL] squash, yellow/crookneck, cubed, boiled, drained
¼ cup [60 mL] kidney beans, cooked, drained
1 tablespoon [15 mL] coconut oil
500 mg calcium from a supplement or slightly more than ¼ teaspoon finely ground eggshell
½ cup [125 mL] broth, if desired

Combine all ingredients, mix well. Serve.

Hint: Coconut oil may need to be warmed slightly to liquefy prior to mixing with food.

🐕 BEEF & ZUCCHINI

Protein: 40 grams **Fat:** 20 grams **Calories:** 410
2 daily servings for a 30 lb dog, can be divided into 4 feedings.

. . . .

1 pound [500 mL] ground beef, 20% fat, cooked
5 ounces [140 mL] beef liver, cubed, cooked (pan-seared)
3 eggs, hard-boiled, sliced
2 cups [500 mL] zucchini, cubed, cooked, drained
6 ounces [150 mL] mushrooms, white, cooked, drained
1 can [460 mL] (14oz can) crushed tomatoes
8 ounces [250 mL] low sodium tomato juice
2 cups [500 mL] spinach, cooked, drained
2 cups [500 mL] black beans, cooked, drained
300 mg calcium from a supplement or slightly less than ¼
    teaspoon finely ground eggshell
Optional: replace tomato juice with 2 cups [500 mL] bone
    broth

Combine all ingredients, mix well. Serve.

Hint: This recipe is great to use up extra summer zucchini.

⚐CHICKEN, SQUASH, ASPARAGUS & GREENS

Protein: 36 grams **Fat:** 28 grams **Calories:** 436
Daily serving for a 30 lb dog, can be divided into 2 feedings.

· ·

½ cup [125 mL] chicken breast, cooked, skin and fat removed, ground or shredded
1 tablespoon [15 mL] chicken liver, cooked, finely chopped
½ cup [125 mL] squash, acorn, cubed, boiled, drained
½ cup [125 mL] asparagus, boiled, drained, chopped
½ cup [125 mL] collard greens, cooked, drained, chopped
1 teaspoon [5 mL] sesame seeds, dried, whole, no salt
1 teaspoon [5 mL] cod liver oil
1 tablespoon [15 mL] coconut oil
500 mg calcium from a supplement or slightly more than ¼ teaspoon finely ground eggshell
½ cup [125 mL] broth, if desired

Combine all ingredients, mix well. Serve.

Hint: Powdered calcium sticks to wet ingredients, sprinkle evenly over wet food.

🐕HEALTHY PAWSIBILITIES BLEND

Protein: 9 grams **Fat:** 2 grams **Calories:** 100
8 servings for a 30 lb dog

. . . .

6 ounces [175 mL] beef liver
6 ounces [175 mL] beef kidney
6 ounces [175 mL] chicken, ground
6 ounces [175 mL] beef, ground
6 ounces [175 mL] turkey, ground
2 tablespoons [30 mL] olive oil
12 ounces [325 mL] cauliflower
12 ounces [325 mL] broccoli
12 ounces [325 mL] carrots
12 ounces [325 mL] red kidney beans, canned or cooked
12 ounces [325 mL] pinto beans, canned or cooked
12 ounces [325 mL] great northern beans, canned or cooked

Mix meats in a large bowl. In large skillet, sauté meats lightly in olive oil, or serve meat raw. Transfer meat to another bowl. In the same large skillet, add vegetables. Cover, turn heat to medium low, and cook until tender. Combine all ingredients, mix well. Serve.

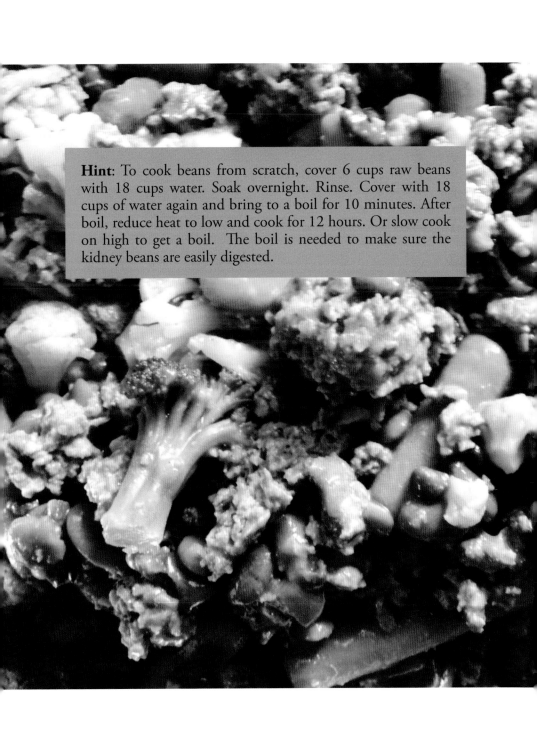

Hint: To cook beans from scratch, cover 6 cups raw beans with 18 cups water. Soak overnight. Rinse. Cover with 18 cups of water again and bring to a boil for 10 minutes. After boil, reduce heat to low and cook for 12 hours. Or slow cook on high to get a boil. The boil is needed to make sure the kidney beans are easily digested.

🐕 SALMON & CABBAGE

Protein: 19 grams **Fat:** 6 grams **Calories:** 230
Daily serving for a 30 lb dog, can be divided into 2 feedings.

. . . .

4 ounces [125 mL] salmon, pink, canned or cooked (leave
  bone), chopped
2 shrimp, medium, cooked
1 egg, hard-boiled, chopped
½ cup [125 mL] cabbage, cooked, drained, shredded
½ cup [125 mL] sweet potato, with skin, boiled or baked,
  chopped
½ cup [125 mL] kidney beans, cooked
300 mg calcium from a supplement or slightly more than ⅛
  teaspoon finely ground eggshell
½ cup [125 mL] broth, if desired

Combine all ingredients, add calcium, mix well. Serve.

Hint: This is a great cooling recipe for dogs who pant a lot.

SPECIAL RECIPES FOR BOTH CATS AND DOGS

Cartilage Soup / Chicken Foot Soup

Cancer Diet

Liver Detoxification Diet

Bone Broth

🐕 CARTILAGE SOUP 🦴
/ CHICKEN FOOT SOUP

Protein: 11 grams **Fat:** 8 grams **Calories:** 120
Portion Size: ½ cup

• •

1 pound [250 mL] chicken feet
2 tablespoons [30 mL] apple cider vinegar

Put chicken feet and vinegar in pot. Cover with water. Bring to a boil. Reduce heat to simmer, cook for about an hour until feet fall apart. Cool. Strain. Refrigerate. This will turn to a thick gelatin. Serve ½ cup with each meal or as a meal to help with aching joints.

Hint: Chicken feet can be purchased at Asian grocery stores.

🐕 CANCER DIET 🐈

Protein: 25 grams **Fat:** 17 grams **Calories:** 270
Portion size: 1 ⅓ cups

• •

2 cups [500 mL] beef, pork or turkey, freshly ground or chopped
1 cup [250 mL] leafy vegetables (kale, spinach, collards), fresh, diced
½ cup [125 mL] raw goat's milk or plain yogurt
¼ cup [60 mL] mushrooms, diced
1 egg, raw
½ apple, diced
½ carrot, shredded
1 clove garlic, minced

Combine all ingredients, it will be like making meatloaf. Store in fridge. Make fresh daily as this mixture can spoil quickly.

Hint: Cancer makes the body hot, and raw meats work best to cool the body that suffers from cancer. However, be extremely careful in your food handling. Use whole cuts of meat and grind it yourself—don't use already ground meat from the grocery store as it's notorious for bacterial contamination. If you can't tolerate raw, either for the gross factor or worry about bacteria, cook the mixture slightly. It's still better than commercially prepared food!

🐕 LIVER DETOXIFICATION DIET

Protein: 25 grams **Fat:** 1 gram **Calories:** 250
Portion size: 1 ½ cups

. . . .

1 ½ cups white potatoes
1 ½ cups sweet potatoes
3 cups mixed zucchini, green beans, celery and other summer
    squash
2 cups white fish (cod, pollack, or similar)

Scrub and cut the potatoes. Place in pot with water to cover. Simmer for 45 minutes. Add the other vegetables and cook for another 10–15 minutes. Add the fish and cook until just cooked through—usually no more than 5 minutes. Serve.

Hint: This diet was formulated by Dr. Jean Dodds to cleanse the liver, for seizure patients on phenobarbital, or simply dogs who have had too much input into their liver over the years.

🐕 BONE BROTH 🐈

Nutritional value depends on bones used. **Never substitute canned broth for this homemade broth**, since canned broths often have a high salt/sodium level.

• •

Bones from previously cooked meats
2 tablespoons [30 mL] apple cider vinegar per pound bones
Water to cover

Place the bones into a slow cooker or large soup pot. Add water to cover the bones. Add cider vinegar (2 tablespoons for each pound of bones). Let stand for 1 hour. Bring to a low boil, reduce heat and simmer for 6 to 12 hours for poultry bones, or 12 to 24 hours for beef bones. Strain broth through a colander or sieve lined with cheesecloth. Discard bones. DO NOT these feed bones to your pet.

Hint: Broth can be refrigerated for 3 days or frozen. Freeze in 1- or 2-cup containers.

TREATS FOR BOTH CATS AND DOGS

Fruity Quickie

Stuffed Celery

Jerky

Almond Butter Cookies

Oat Cookies

Liver Treats

Pumpkin Biscuit

Yogurt Drops

🐕 FRUITY QUICKIE

Protein: 2 grams **Fat:** 1 gram **Calories:** 140

• •

½ banana, apple, pear or
1 cup [250 mL] blueberries, mixed fruit or
¼ cup [60 mL] dried hawthorne berries (great treat or topper
    for heart conditions)
¼ cup [60 mL] fresh bitter melon (great treat for diabetics)

Peel banana and serve. For the other fruits, wash and serve.

Hint: If you have more time, slice the fruit and dehydrate. Keep refrigerated until used. Remember, one cup fresh fruit will shrink quite a bit, so don't overfeed dehydrated fruit.

To dehydrate in a commercial dehydrator, spread fruit or layer thick on trays, with space between fruits for air drying. Every 4 hours, rotate trays so the top tray moves closer to the fan/heat source. Fruit is dry/done when leathery and removed easily from the tray without being burned.

To dehydrate in your oven, place a cake rack on a cookie sheet. Spread fruit one layer thick with space in between pieces. Turn oven to lowest temperature possible—usually 200–250 degrees pieces. Every 4 hours, check fruit to see if it's leathery and easy to remove from the cake rack.

🐕 STUFFED CELERY

Protein: 3 grams **Fat:** 9 grams **Calories:** 100
Serving size: one half stalk of stuffed celery per day.

· ·

½ stalk celery
1 tablespoon [15 mL] almond butter

Separate each stalk from the bunch. Wash and dry. Spreat nut butter in the celery stalk.

Optionally, you can slice the stuffed celery into small bites for small dogs.

Wrap and place in freezer until frozen. Serve frozen for a fun treat.

Hint: Yes, you can eat this too!

🐕 JERKY 🐈

Nutritional value depends on meat used

. . . .

Chicken breast or flank steak

Trim off the fat. Place meat in the freezer for 30-60 minutes so it becomes firm—this makes it easier to cut. Cut ¼-inch strips across the grain. Either place in a dehydrator or an oven on low (200 degrees). It will take 4–6 hours depending on how thick you cut the slices. Rotate trays, turn the meat. When chewy, remove, cool then store in fridge.

Hint: If you like to camp, make extra and bring some for yourself!

⋔ ALMOND BUTTER COOKIES

Protein: 6 grams **Fat:** 8 grams **Calories:** 190

. . . .

2 cups [500 mL] carrot, raw, grated
½ cup [125 mL] parsley, fresh, chopped
¼ cup [60 mL] olive oil, extra virgin
3 ⅓ cups [875 mL] whole wheat flour
3 tablespoons [45 mL] almond butter

Preheat oven to 325 degrees. Combine ingredients into a dough. Roll out on a floured surface ¼-inch thick. Cut into 1-inch squares for dogs, ¼ inch squares for cats and place on a cookie sheet. Bake for 20–30 minutes. Allow to cool completely before serving.

Hint: Try grated zucchini in the summer time.

OAT COOKIES

Protein: 6 grams **Fat:** 9 grams **Calories:** 200

• •

1 ¼ cups [315 mL] whole wheat flour
1 ½ cups [375 mL] wheat bread flour
1 cup [250 mL] oats, dry
½ cup [125 mL] pumpkin seeds
4 tablespoons [60 mL] coconut oil
¾ cup [175 mL] bone broth or chicken stock, no salt added

Preheat oven to 325 degrees. Mix the flours, oats, pumpkin seeds, coconut oil and broth. Mix thoroughly.

For dogs: Scoop 1 tablespoon at a time. Shape into a ball and place 1-inch apart on a baking sheet.

For cats: Spread dough flat on baking sheet. Use a butter knife to cut through every ¼–½ inch, making a grid of small, crunchy bites for cat mouths.

Bake for 40 minutes, turn off heat and allow to harden in the oven for 60 minutes.

Hint: Store in the freezer for long-term storage of big batches!

🐕 LIVER TREATS 🐈

Protein: 6 grams **Fat:** 3.5 grams **Calories:** 90

. . . .

1 pound [250 mL] chicken, lamb or beef liver
1 cup [250 mL] skim milk
2 cups [500 mL] flour (try 1 cup brown rice flour and 1 cup
    oat flour)
3 tablespoons [45 mL] olive oil
2 raw eggs
2 tablespoons [45 mL] dry parsley

Purée the liver and milk in a blender until smooth. Mix flour, oil, eggs and parsley in a bowl. Fold the liver purée into the mixture and stir until ingredients form a smooth paste. Pour into a greased 9x13 pan and bake at 350 degrees for 30–35 minutes. Treats are done when a toothpick pulls out of treats clean.

Keep what will be used for 3–4 days in the refrigerator, place the remainder in several small containers and freeze until needed.

Hint: these are great to hide pills in.

🐕 PUMPKIN 🐈 BISCUITS

Protein: 4 grams **Fat:** 2 grams **Calories:** 140

. . . .

2 raw eggs
½ cup [125 mL] canned pumpkin
2 tablespoons [30 mL] cheddar cheese
¼ teaspoon [1 mL] sea salt
1 teaspoon [5 mL] dried parsley
2 ½ cups [625 mL] brown rice flour

Preheat oven to 350 degrees. Whisk together eggs and pumpkin. Stir in cheese, salt and parsley. Add flour gradually, combining with spatula or hands (dough will be very stiff). Turn out onto lightly floured surface. Roll to ¼-inch thick. Use cookie cutters to cut shapes. Place on ungreased cookie sheets. Bake for 20 minutes. Remove from oven. Carefully turn over with a spatula. Return to oven and bake for an additional 20 minutes. Cool on a rack.

Hint: When in season, fresh pumpkin works well too! And, pumpkin is great for diarrhea.

🐕 YOGURT DROPS 🐈

Protein: 1 gram **Fat:** 1.5 grams **Calories:** 20

. . . .

Yogurt, plain
Blueberries, or other berries

Line baking sheet with parchment paper. By spoonfuls, plop yogurt onto parchment paper, leaving enough room between the plops that they won't run together. Place a blueberry in the center of each yogurt plop. Freeze.

Hint: Serve frozen on warm summer days.

ABOUT THE AUTHORS

Dr. Cathy Alinovi is a holistic veterinarian, pet lover, frequent media guest, and nationally-celebrated author. Dr. Cathy knew she wanted to be an animal doctor since she was nine years old. Her mission then was simple: to make the world safe for dogs. Her mission now—providing healthy options for pets, allowing them to live longer and with a better quality of life—is not much different, and is just as powerful! Relentlessly committed to her patients' care, Dr. Cathy is quickly gaining national recognition for her integrative approach to animal health.

Dr. Cathy began her veterinary education at Purdue University School of Veterinary Medicine and also holds a Master of Science in Epidemiology from Purdue, but quickly realized that conventional medicine met some, but not enough, of her patients' needs.

So, she went back to school and became certified in animal chiropractic care. And, of course, her passionate commitment to animal health wouldn't let her stop there. Since then, she has also become certified in veterinary food therapy, veterinary acupuncture, Chinese herbal therapy, and aromatherapy.

When asked what training is next, Dr. Cathy says, "Whatever my patients need me to learn." Dr. Cathy is the owner and veterinarian of Healthy PAWsibilities, an integrative veterinary clinic in rural Pine Village, Indiana. Dr Cathy offers in-clinic and virtual health consultations to her patients all over the world through her website at www.healthypawsibilities.com.

She treats 80% of what walks through the door not with expensive prescriptions but with adequate nutrition. The heart of every exam within her office includes "the food talk." To help her clients on the path to good food, she co-authored this book, *Dinner PAWsible*, a pet food cookbook that uses human-grade ingredients to make yummy balanced meals for pets at half the cost of commercial pet food. These easy-to-make recipes please both dog and cat palates, can work to help stop shedding and treat "leaky gut" issues which are common in most of her patients.

Susan Thixton, dubbed the "Caped Crusader for Safe Pet Food," is a pet food safety advocate.

Susan's pet food education began almost twenty years ago when her beloved dog was diagnosed with bone cancer. Even worse news came when Susan's trusted veterinarian told her that the chemical preservative ethoxyquin, found in her dog's food, was the likely cause of the cancer. Her vet explained that the chemical preservative was used to extend the shelf life of dog food. One phone call later to the pet food manufacturer (the leading dog food brand in the United States at the time) changed Susan's life. The pet food company told Susan that, with ethoxyquin, their dog food would remain fresh for twenty-five years! This was more than three times as long as Susan's dog had lived.

Today, Susan is the publisher of the website TruthaboutPetFood.com and founder of the pet food consumer advocacy group Association for Truth in Pet Food. Susan holds advisor positions on two Association of American Feed Control Officials (AAFCO) committees (a pet food regulatory association) and represents the voices of consumers with the Food and Drug Administration (FDA).

To learn more about commercial pet food, read Susan's first book *Buyer Beware, The Crimes, Lies, and Truth about Pet Food* and subscribe to the free newsletter on TruthaboutPetFood.com.

INDEX